MODERN TRAINS and SPLENDID STATIONS

EDITED BY MARTHA THORNE

MODERN TRAINS and SPLENDID STATIONS

ARCHITECTURE, DESIGN, AND RAIL TRAVEL FOR THE TWENTY-FIRST CENTURY

MERRELL | THE ART INSTITUTE OF CHICAGO

First published in 2001 by
Merrell Publishers Limited
42 Southwark Street
London SE1 1UN

This book accompanies
Modern Trains and Splendid Stations:
Architecture, Design, and Rail Travel for the Twenty-First Century,
an exhibition held at

The Art Institute of Chicago
111 South Michigan Avenue
Chicago, IL 60603
December 8, 2001 – July 29, 2002

Distributed in the USA and Canada
by Rizzoli International Publications, Inc.
through St. Martin's Press, 175 Fifth Avenue, New York,
NY 10010

British Library Cataloguing-in-Publication Data
Thorne, Martha
Modern trains and splendid stations : architecture, design, and
rail travel for the twenty-first century
1.Railroad stations – design and construction 2.Architecture,
Modern – 20th century 3.High speed trains – design and
construction
I.Title
725.3'1'09045

ISBN 1 85894 149 0

Produced by Merrell Publishers Limited
Designed by Maggi Smith
Edited by Richard Dawes

Printed and bound in Italy

CONTENTS

PREFACE

I have always been passionate about railways. Whether traveling down on the amazing vertiginous route from the rainforest behind Cairns in Australia on the Kuranda Scenic Railway or riding the Shinkansen from Tokyo to Osaka, the experience of simply being on a train nearly always surpasses other forms of travel. Not always, of course. The quality varies enormously. How does one assess the quality of a journey? Perhaps one starts with the station or maybe even further back than that—to where the station is situated. Many fine railway stations are set in great spaces such as in Milan, Helsinki, or Venice. Most great terminals are at the heart of cities, allowing one the huge advantage of traveling easily from city center to city center.

Turning to stations themselves rather than their settings, it seems reasonable to separate "through stations" from the great city terminals. Although new terminals are becoming more rare as major "through stations" such as Berlin and Cologne are being projected, it is terminals we look to for great works of architecture and it is these great stations that are featured prominently in this book.

The great terminals such as Paddington and St Pancras in London, the Gare du Nord and the Gare d'Austerlitz in Paris, and perhaps our own Waterloo International in London (see pp. 16–17), all strive to become great heroic environments. Not only are there lofty train sheds (which, incidentally, originally allowed for the dispersion of smoke and now of diesel fumes as well as providing space for overhead electric power lines), but also, in a civilized way, restaurants, cafés, news stands, and all the support services that a traveler needs. They also provide the major thing that the air traveler is without: the ability to arrive by taxi, tube, metro, or on foot only ten minutes before departure. Waiting times at airports combined with the fact that they are always well away from city centers means that for many journeys it is quicker to travel from city center to city center by train.

This is certainly the case for the journey from our Eurostar Terminal at Waterloo to Paris, where the journey reliably and regularly takes no more than three hours by train with twenty minutes at Waterloo and the Gare du Nord. By air the uncertainties are numerous. The roads to Heathrow and into Paris are heavily congested, and even using the Heathrow Express and the RER, the quicker transfer times do not compensate for the long check-in times and the inevitable air-traffic-control delays.

If the "quality-of-life" aspects of train travel versus travel by car, coach, or plane are taken into account, then train travel wins hands down. The ability to board the train ten minutes beforehand, have wonderful countryside views, eat well (this is still only a potential until dining cars can be franchised to top restaurants!), do serious work (I have heard of a Queen's Counsel lawyer who lives in Paris and commutes on a regular basis to London's Law Courts), and be almost certain of arrival on time really outweighs any other form of transport. There is also the very important aspect of environmental damage. Clean and efficient electrically powered trains compare very well with environmentally polluting planes and vehicles, and the energy use per passenger kilometer is substantially less than for air or automobile travel. (Only buses use fuel more efficiently but they are still major pollutants of the atmosphere.)

It is quite possible that, with the right government incentives, Europe could become a "plane-free zone" within the next quarter of a century, as could many other compact zones of the world such as Korea, Japan, and parts of the U.S. Air transport could then be concentrated on truly international routes, with the "quality of life" improving both at airports and on the (probably double-deck) planes, which will incorporate sleeping quarters, gyms, and even, possibly, good food!

I can envisage a fast, efficient train system throughout Europe with seating as good as any vehicle, with audio-visual and computer links, with bookable meeting rooms, high-quality food, exercise facilities, and sleeping cars for the longer journeys.

Entertainment is also a possibility with on-board casinos, cinemas, and even roving musicians and conjurors.

If all this is to be achieved, a fundamental change in attitude is needed. The French railway system, which is the best in Europe, has been achieved only by very heavy government investment coupled with a complete faith in the value of rail travel. As I write this, the French have just opened their route to Marseille, and the first train has traveled from Calais to Marseille, a journey of some 600 miles, in three hours. This is surely train travel at its grandest and most convenient. By contrast, the Green Party in Germany is objecting to new railway building on environmental grounds, claiming that people travel unnecessarily and should stay at home and communicate electronically! They do have a point here, and working from home is going to affect travel habits fundamentally in the next twenty-five years. However, people will still need to travel to meet face to face and to satisfy their need to experience different places and different cultures. Surely it is better to do this by train and long-distance international flights than by covering more and more of our planet with tarmac roads and polluting vehicles?

Of course there are going to be international differences here. It is going to be very difficult to pry a German or US citizen from his automobile unless train travel can offer at least an equivalent in comfort and speed. Furthermore, feeder systems of branch lines (which, in many instances, will need to be re-opened), tramways, and minibuses will have to be developed of equal standard of comfort if the average car driver is to be truly convinced.

Finally it will be very, very important to ensure that stations do not turn into airports—which many people describe these days as being supermarkets with planes parked in the parking lot!

Most of the stations in this book do have splendor and quality and will indeed encourage the excitement of arrival and the exhilaration of departure—the words we used in our original presentation on Waterloo International. However, there is a delicate balance that needs to be maintained. The stations

must be of high architectural quality in order to attract a whole new range of passengers. No compromise should take place here. No design-and-build "value-engineered" schemes should be allowed.

The trains also must remain of good quality in order to attract passengers from their cars. Compromise here would be disastrous. If new trains become crowded and cramped with bad facilities then the surge in people using them will not continue.

This book is a celebration of the good things that are happening in station architecture and train design. I hope it will be an inspiration to all.

Nicholas Grimshaw
June 2001

FOREWORD

Railway stations of the nineteenth century have long been called the cathedrals of the Industrial Revolution. As public spaces that drew together crowds of people of all social strata, the great rail terminals of the Victorian era, with their imposing head buildings and impressive glass-covered sheds, inspired an awe equaled only by that created by the soaring vaults and architectonic massing of cathedrals. They also established themselves at the very center of commerce, communication, and culture, representing, as they do in Claude Monet's paintings of Gare St-Lazare in Paris, the dynamism of modern life.

Though such stations may never regain the height of their cultural significance, we are once again enjoying an era during which exciting new train stations are being constructed in many different countries by world-renowned architects. These new buildings have expanded missions, many times providing facilities for several modes of travel under one roof. Some celebrate the technological potential of high-speed rail; others have the ambitious goal of serving as catalysts for urban renewal. The design of trains themselves has also evolved significantly: they provide comfort and accessibility to passengers with a variety of purposes in traveling. Few fields of industrial design are as complex, seeking to solve issues of technology, safety, comfort, and beauty with rolling stock that must serve the public for many years of intensive use.

This is the third and final segment of a trilogy of projects undertaken by the Department of Architecture since 1996, focusing on the topic of transportation in architecture and design. Following upon the success of *Building for Air Travel: Architecture and Design for Commercial Aviation* (1996) and *2001: Building for Space Travel* (2001), The Art Institute of Chicago seeks to demonstrate that the field of architecture is broad and encompasses the allied disciplines of design, engineering, technology, and urban and regional planning. As always, this book and the exhibition it accompanies recognize achievements of remarkable quality that touch vast numbers of people in their everyday lives.

James N. Wood
Director and President
The Art Institute of Chicago

9

MARTHA THORNE

RENAISSANCE OF THE TRAIN STATION

Waterloo International Terminal, London, Nicholas Grimshaw and Partners, detail of roof interior

The design of train stations is one of the most complex and large-scale challenges facing architects today. Few building types must provide the kind of physical infrastructure required for such a dynamic activity as rail travel. Stations must serve a large number of temporary users—users whose needs, purposes of travel, time spent in the station, and demographic profiles vary enormously.

Although the critic John Ruskin experienced rail travel at its inception, he nonetheless described in 1849, with his customary insightfulness, its persistent challenges: "The whole system of railway travelling is addressed to people who, being in a hurry, are therefore for the time being miserable. No one would travel in that manner who could help it."[1] Passengers ever since have uttered the same sentiments. The history of train travel has, of course, experienced highs and lows, and these shifts make its study all the more demanding. It is especially interesting to attempt to view the current state of the art, because it appears that we are at the beginning stages of a buoyant new period of train-station design.

The history of the train station dates back to the early nineteenth century. According to Carroll Meeks, whose book *The Railroad Station* (1956) remains one of the most complete texts on the architectural history and interpretation of the passenger terminal,

"There was no functional precedent for the [first] depot; every solution had to be invented. The station was an essential part of the new system of transportation; it reflected the impact of the technology and mobility of the masses."[2]

The creation of the modern railway occurred almost simultaneously in the U.S.A. and Great Britain. Both the Liverpool to Manchester railway and the Baltimore and Ohio line opened in 1830. The first British station was built in Liverpool. The simple wooden shed that was erected there and used for a few years naturally no longer exists. In Baltimore, Maryland, meanwhile, the Mount Clare station of 1830 was a small office with no train shed at all. It has been estimated that in the period from 1830 through 1950, 40,000 passenger stations were constructed.[3] These were of all types, from the modest building with a single platform to the great terminal in major cities.

Train-station architecture developed quickly in response to the rapid growth in rail travel, which became a universal means of transporting goods and products from one place to another. The station was converted into the "temple of technology" where passengers anxiously awaited one of the most important inventions of the Industrial Revolution. In the middle of the nineteenth century two

St. Pancras Station, London

programmatic components could be identified for most stations and required their own architecture: first, a shed to cover the trains and protect those who worked on them; and, second, an attached building for ticketing and servicing passengers; offices for railway management and employees; and, as Ruskin would have expected, a waiting room. The building for passengers could be located on one side of the shed, both sides, or in a head building. Although wood was sometimes used to form the trusses that supported the roof of the shed, iron and glass became the predominant materials for this purpose, a logical development of the times that had a vast impact on the application of this construction technology to the architecture of numerous other building types.

As the nineteenth century progressed, so did rail travel. The second half of the century was a period of improvement in matters of safety, speed, and comfort. Sleeping cars, dining cars, air brakes, electric foot warmers, and other inventions became common parts of train sets. Within the stations, what is now known as the concourse became a standard feature. Offices, waiting rooms, ticket facilities, and other services for travelers were grouped together in increasingly impressive spaces. The concourse was first developed in terminus stations, placed between the stub-end tracks and the street, as in the case of Gare de l'Est in Paris of 1852 by François Duquesney. Certain railway companies believed the inclusion of

a hotel within a station would also facilitate travel and respond to the needs and demands of travelers. Thus buildings such as the Grosvenor Hotel, next to Victoria Station (1861), and the Charing Cross Hotel (1865), adjacent to that station, were built in London.

During the 1860s the length and span of the roofs covering train sheds grew, attesting to the capabilities of the engineers who participated in the design and construction of stations. The Neuer Bahnhof in Stuttgart (1868) had a total span of 61.6 meters and a length of 165 meters. Porta Nuova Station in Turin (1868) also reached 165 meters long, with a total span of 47 meters. Often, however, there was little integration of the parts of the station. Indeed, it almost appears as if there was conflict between the architects and engineers. In the case of St. Pancras Station in London, for example, the shed, with a total span of 73 meters and a length of 209 meters, was designed even before the architect of the station building, Sir George Gilbert Scott, had been selected. The shed roof, designed by engineer William Henry Barlow with R.M. Ordish and completed in 1868, was the longest span attempted to that date. Scott brought to the project a neo-Gothic style, articulated with towers and pinnacles to form a counterpoint to the rest of the adjacent structure, and completed the station in 1873.

The period from the third quarter of the nineteenth century through 1915 could rightfully be considered the era of the great train shed. The use

Union Station, Cincinnati, Ohio,
Fellheimer and Wagner

of glass and iron to cover large areas was not limited just to stations; exhibitions halls, markets, and arcades employed similar systems: the Crystal Palace in London by Sir Joseph Paxton (1851), Les Halles market in Paris by Victor Baltard (1870), the Paris Exposition of 1878, and the World's Columbian Exposition of 1893 in Chicago had various exhibition buildings that successfully combined glass and iron. The triumphs of engineering for long-span, lightweight structures were beautifully expressed in the most practical of structures: bridges, tunnels, greenhouses, and, of course, train stations. Multiple examples remain to inspire us: Pennsylvania Station at Broad Street in Philadelphia (1893) was the largest single-span train shed in the world at that time, with 91.5 meters. But the larger Frankfurt am Main station by Eggert and Faust (1888), with its three-span shed with a total width of 169 meters and a length of 188 meters, and the 1915 Leipzig Station by architects Lossow and Kuhne and engineer Louis Eilers, with eight separate spans for a total width of over 300 meters, continue to serve their original purposes quite well.

Even if most great train stations included impressive sheds and often other identifiable elements such as a tower and overhanging porch or canopy, the architectural styles employed by architects for the main building were varied. The functions of stations, it can be argued, developed similarly in many places at the same time, although the styles chosen for station buildings were diverse. The choice was linked not only to the predominant style of the day, but in some cases to the expression of corporate pride through their buildings. For Union Station in St. Louis, Missouri, Theodore Link and Edward Cameron in 1894 chose a grand Gothic tower and melded it with a Romanesque vocabulary inspired by H.H. Richardson. The Beaux-Arts style that was popular in the early twentieth century made its appearance in numerous stations in France and the U.S.A., including Gare d'Orsay in Paris (1900) and Grand Central Station in New York (1913).

If the most significant numbers of grand stations were built during the final decades of the nineteenth century and the first ones of the twentieth, later periods still produced other architecturally significant examples of stations, though their numbers are perhaps not as numerous as in previous decades. While traditional elements of station design continued to appear, a new vocabulary was clearly emerging. Central Station in Milan, begun in 1913 and completed in 1930, was a final example of the "grand station" of monumental proportions and imagery. Helsinki Station (1914), by the firm Saarinen, Gesellius and Lindgren, evolved from an early, historically determined, "romantic" notion with medieval-style towers to a much freer, modern idiom with a more forward-looking architectural character. Although Saarinen incorporated one great clock tower, an entrance canopy, and a single entry arch, his stylistic language

Railroad Station, Helsinki,
Finland, Eliel Saarinen

was much more a precursor to Art Deco elements than it was reminiscent of past styles. The era of the great train shed was also supplanted with other materials, techniques, and architectural details. In the U.S.A., Union Station in Cincinnati, Ohio, by Fellheimer and Wagner, completed in 1933, presented an extremely functional design scheme, but with a monumental arch that created a gateway between the city and station. But the architectural language chosen was Art Deco, internationally popular in the late 1920s. The rich interior is due to the hand of architect Paul Cret of Philadelphia.

Modernism was also adopted for some great stations, especially in Germany, Italy, and The Netherlands. Termini Station in Rome, begun by Angiolo Mazzoni and completed in 1951 by rationalist architect Eugenio Montuori, featured a classically inspired colonnade attached to the front of a rather plain modernist structure. H.G. Schelling's Amstel Station in Amsterdam (1940) was a simple, glass-enclosed building for the main space and lower complementary wings for office functions.

With the end of the Second World War, train service began to suffer a steady decline. Even if it provided an efficient and economically viable mode of transport for certain markets, namely mass commuters in large metropolitan areas or the transport of freight on some routes, nonetheless the writing on the wall indicated that the future development of train travel was not assured. The automobile was most definitely the main competitor in the U.S.A. and Germany as well as to some degree in other European countries. Cars were fast, comfortable, provided "door-to-door" service, and were affordable for the growing middle class. For long distances, air travel was providing stiff competition. All this, coupled with a lack of clear and constant support from political spheres and only modest investments in infrastructure, along with the pause in the development of train technology during the war, meant that railways faced a huge challenge. And stations, too, reflected this lack of enthusiasm and commitment. Few were built, and those that were were often less than inspiring examples of architecture.

The task to recuperate train travel's previous glory would prove a monumental challenge. Industry understood that speed was a critical factor in improving the position of the rail transit and this was directly related to technology. The French can be considered the first to begin methodical research, as far back as 1950, into increasing the threshold of speed. In 1962, the limit was at 160 kph. German's federal railway, Deutsche Bahn, was the first to operate trains regularly at that limit. The Germans were soon to find out, however, as the French did, that the improvement of trains sets had to go hand in hand with the improvement of the tracks. Otherwise, the gains in speed were wiped out by losses in safety and deterioration of tracks and excessive, uneven wear to the wheels. A retreat was made and investigation continued. The lines of research included the introduction of continuously welded rail sections. To respond to the limitation of existing track that often was not conducive to constantly maintained high speed, research branched off into lightening the weight of trains and developing new forms of running gear that would ease the stress on the old tracks. Tilting systems that would tilt vehicle bodies and allow curves to be taken at faster speeds was another area of development. In Spain, the manufacturing company Talgo worked on concepts of minimal weight of cars with a low center of gravity and a suspension and wheel system that ease trains through curves. Italy's industries developed the Pendolino tilting train.

By the 1970s and early 1980s there were many successful examples of improved rail technologies at the service of the passenger, especially in Europe and Japan. The Talgo "pendular," which could reach speeds of up to 200 kph, was used throughout the Spanish network in the early 1980s. The French in 1976 began the construction of the LGV (Lignes à Grande Vitesse), a new dedicated track for high-speed rail. By 1983 Paris and Lyon were only about two hours apart for trains averaging speeds of approximately 214 kph. Now rail travel could compete with air travel in terms of time, but also save energy, about 60% per passenger per kilometer over certain types of aircraft.

The Japanese gave a clear push to rail travel with the introduction of the Shinkansen trains in 1964. These "bullet trains" could run regularly and consistently at speeds of just over 200 kph. Japan built exclusive-use tracks from Tokyo to Osaka. The network was to grow over the years, although it was not always a smooth expansion, and today is a complete system of over 3000 kilometers.

Without a doubt, the improved technology, increased ridership, and a projected future growth of train-travel demand led to an increased need for new stations. It has been commonly observed that railway architecture has been experiencing a "renaissance" since the 1980s. This resurgence can be directly traced to technological improvements, one of which is the development of high-speed rail travel. This factor, though extremely important, is only one of the reasons that attention has turned back to trains. Others that have contributed to the increasing momentum that rail travel is gathering include a generalized response to the increasing traffic jams and deficiencies of other modes of travel, namely airlines and the private car for certain routes. The oil crisis of the early 1970s helped focus attention back toward mass transit as an economic means of travel. Other specific factors that have played a part in the rejuvenation of rail travel include: the formation of the European Community; a response to the destruction and demolition of many great stations of the Railway Age during the 1960s; large-scale international events; special political or development

Waterloo International Terminal, London, Nicholas Grimshaw and Partners, train exit

Waterloo International Terminal, London, Nicholas Grimshaw and Partners, passenger waiting area

opportunities; and the increased role of architects in contributing to a new awareness of station architecture.

The breaking down of barriers through the formation of the European Community has led to more discussion, and to coordination of the various rail networks in Europe. Industry-wide standards for trains, safety, maintenance, and joint-investment projects have contributed to new and improved service in many places and subsequently the construction of new stations. The document on the European High Speed Rail Network issued in 1989 called for plans for 9000 kilometers of new track and 15,000 kilometers of upgraded track, which would increase ridership fourfold between 1995 and 2025. Perhaps the most identifiable project that increased the closeness of countries was the building of the Channel Tunnel link between Great Britain and the Continent. This very prominent step in a united Europe had its antecedent decades before the opening of the tunnel in 1992. As early as 1802, in fact, a proposal was put forward to link Britain and France by a wood-framed shaft, ventilated by projecting chimneys and served by horse-drawn express coaches. At the 1867 World's Fair in Paris, the two countries jointly displayed a scheme for a rail tunnel to link Calais and Dover. The completion of the Channel Tunnel 125 years later was not only a remarkable feat of engineering, but also a test of diplomacy and a victory for train travel.

The agreement first signed between France and Great Britain in 1973 produced an initial phase of construction that saw 400 meters dug by 1975, when the British government pulled out of the agreement for financial reasons. A renewed accord was reached in 1985, with plans this time calling for private financing of the tunnel. Work resumed on the Channel Tunnel, and, in the end, three separate tunnels were opened: two for trains running in opposite directions, and a service tunnel between them. To handle the increased rail traffic into and out of this region and the introduction of the Eurostar train – a new high-speed rail service connecting London with Paris and Brussels – a new terminal at Waterloo Station in London was undertaken.

In 1988, the firm of Nicholas Grimshaw and Partners was commissioned to design the new rail facility at Waterloo. The new terminus is located adjacent to the existing station. The only available site for expansion was hemmed in by the alignment of the existing tracks and the narrowness of the site. The architects also faced the challenge of handling efficiently the 15,000,000 passengers projected to use this facility each year. The new terminal has four levels and is crowned by a spectacular sloping roof, creating a modern-day train shed reminiscent in form of great earlier examples, but also in its ability to inspire passengers and architects alike. From the lowest level, containing parking facilities, one moves up to the arrival area, above which are departure

Two views of model for Abando Intermodal Passenger Station, Bilbao, Spain, Michael Wilford and Partners Ltd.

lounges, and finally, the boarding platforms at the uppermost level. The station sought to accommodate passengers, allowing them to move quickly and easily through the facility. Easy orientation and a view toward the sleek Eurostar trains were other goals reflected in the design.

The new terminal would probably not have been built were it not for the demands placed on it by the Eurostar high-speed train. Nonetheless, the creation of a station that is more than the sum of its functional properties, that is, in fact, a stunning symbol of progress and a lasting monument for the city, is directly related to the power of its architecture. Grimshaw's station can be seen as an emblem of the railway renaissance in terms of both improved travel and high-quality architecture. The boldness of his design and the uncompromising search for an appropriate and celebratory language for the architecture of stations without a doubt did much to put station architecture back in the public and professional area for discussion and recognition. No station has been so widely acclaimed in both popular and professional media. It was one of the first such major projects to illustrate that architecture can fulfill multiple goals in an efficient yet innovative way.

Other outstanding international firms have been called upon to design major transit stations. Citing only winners of the prestigious Pritzker Architecture Prize who have undertaken rail facilities creates an impressive list: Renzo Piano for the subway system in

Genoa (1983–91) and the office of James Stirling and Michael Wilford for an unrealized project for Bilbao, Spain, first commissioned in 1990; as well as Sir Norman Foster (see pp. 62–66) and Rafael Moneo (see pp. 127–29). Although it can be argued that, on certain levels, the decision to hire a famous architect is also an attempt to garner publicity through the "star system" of famous names, there is no denying that these very same architects, however internationally famous they may be, have designed some of the most thoughtful and successful stations. It says much for both the public and private institutions that participate in selection processes that they have sought out "the best and the brightest" professionals for the tasks at hand, thus recognizing both the short- and the long-term importance of the train station.

International events such as the Olympic Games and international expositions often function as the catalyst to new development, including improved transport facilities. This was true even in history. The opening of Gare d'Orsay was to coincide with the Paris Exposition of 1900. Recent examples of the key role that transport stations play in special-event plans include Seville (and indirectly Madrid) and Lisbon. Both cities have undertaken new stations to serve international expositions. Although the timetable and location were carefully coordinated with the event, the station was planned for its long-term use by the residents of the cities. In the case of

Santa Justa Station (see pp. 130–33), the new station was the result of the first high-speed rail line in Spain, constructed between Madrid and Seville. The opportunity to showcase Seville with an event that would attract approximately 40,000,000 visitors over a six-month period gave the impetus needed to undertake major changes. The station was, however, also part of a larger plan to eliminate the grade crossings, thereby reconnecting the city's fabric and the river, and to reorganize a significant part of the city. It was also seen as the magnet for development of an area of the city and set an example for other projects to coordinate with growth in public transportation.

Oriente Station in Lisbon (see pp. 120–23) is part of the overall redevelopment plans of Lisbon to change an area bordering the sea, west of the city center. Built in what was previously an industrial area of Lisbon, the International Exposition would provide the short-term rationale for new infrastructure and urban services that would ultimately transform an obsolete area of the city into one more appropriate for the coming century. It is reasonable to assume that future celebrations will continue to combine transport needs with the desire to be a showcase for the world.

Although Berlin in some ways may be a unique instance within Europe, it provides an interesting case study on the importance that architecture and transportation networks have for the configuration of a city. It also shows a political commitment to public transportation instead of just a promotion of private automobile travel. Two concepts for an overall transportation plan for Berlin were originally discussed: a circular model, similar to a ring road, to distribute trains entering the city from the north or south; and a plan based on the intersection of north–south and east–west lines at one point and subsequent linkages with the suburban and urban (S-Bahn and U-Bahn) transport systems. The second idea was adapted and accepted, giving rise to Lehrter Bahnhof, a major but not single central station. Located in an underdeveloped area of the city, it became the keystone of a larger development plan that would create a new district adjacent to the new government quarter. The new station (see pp. 78–81) is a multipurpose center that has as its goal the integration of urban design, transport, economic, and service systems. The architecture is one of optimism for a city of the future: modern, technological. The transportation functions are neither accentuated nor hidden, but are an integral part of the development.

Eurolille, a new city center for Lille, symbolizes a new round of urban initiatives in France. In the 1980s, a renewed emphasis on the decentralization of government and increased roles for local authorities, along with a need for repositioning urban areas within a framework of a united Europe, led to aggressive urban strategies for some regional cities. The master plan, the result of a competition, was designed by Rem Koolhaas and his Office for Metropolitan Architecture (OMA). Previous to the master plan, it was assumed that the train station would be located outside the city. Following a series of discussions between various levels of government and the national French railway agency (SNCF), the station was moved to the city center. The initial proposals had sited the TGV underground, running through a tunnel, virtually invisible in the city. The final plan, however, brought a radical change: the importance of the train and the entire transportation system was celebrated, not hidden, and it made the

station a very visible anchor for Eurolille. This station (see pp. 72–73), which has as its strongest symbolic component the wave-like roof, seeks to blend the activities inside and outside the station, making it a place of many activities, not just an arrival or departure point.

Train service is increasingly linking airports with major cities, and often this means new stations adjacent to airport terminals, as can be seen by examples such as Frankfurt Airport ICE-Railway Station or Cologne-Bonn Station in Germany, and Inchon International Airport Station in Korea. A major effort linking air travel and rail travel has been undertaken in Hong Kong. The new Hong Kong International Airport, which officially opened in 1998, was one of the largest projects in civil-engineering history. Massive earth-moving and reclamation operations created a 1248-hectare site for the new airport, designed by Foster and Partners with Arup as engineering partners. The new airport express line provides mass transit between the airport, Kowloon and Hong Kong and creates seven new stations. All three stations, Hong Kong, Kowloon and Tsing Yi, are part of much larger commercial developments, with the rail service at the core. These are only a few of the many examples that indicate the complementary potential of rail and air travel.

Although an analysis of train-station renovations is outside the scope of this work, it is worth recognizing the great efforts that preservations have

Inch'on Airport Station, South Korea,
Terry Farrell and Partners

View of central hall, Musée d'Orsay, Paris

made toward saving outstanding examples of station architecture.[6] These efforts have contributed to raising the public's consciousness about the rich heritage of this type of building and have refocused attention on station architecture in general. Through the work and support of not-for-profit groups, such as the Railway Heritage Trust, founded in Britain in 1984, and, more recently, the Great American Station Foundation, dating from 1996, numerous stations have been preserved. Often they experience adaptive reuse as exhibitions halls and in other roles. Gare d'Orsay, in Paris, is a most significant example of a train station becoming a major museum. Union Station in St. Louis, Missouri, has become a retail and hotel complex. Many times, as in the case of

Grand Central Station in New York City, Union Station in Washington, D.C., and 30th Street Station in Philadelphia, to pick three examples in the U.S.A., or the Estación de Francia (France Station) in Barcelona and many examples in Italy, buildings designed originally as major train stations continue to serve their transport function in a renewed and beautiful way.

If the nineteenth century was the century of the train and the twentieth century was that of the airplane and the automobile, could it be that the twenty-first century will be the age of more attention to the needs of the train passenger? Certainly the railroad industry is changing: its uses, potential passengers, and goals are no longer as limited as

Lyon-Satolas Station, France,
Santiago Calatrava, view of roof

in the past. High-speed rail is the preferred form of transport on certain routes. The ease of traveling from city center to city center, avoiding long waiting periods at airport, could contribute to an increased demand for rail service. Station planners are trying to see trains as part of a broader network of transportation modes. Rail lines can now hook up more rationally with airports, bus stations, and even car parks. The move to the suburbs has put increasing demand on the train as a viable link with the center of cities. In some suburban communities the station, not the town hall or church, is the new focal point of the community.

Stations must therefore respond to different objectives than in the past. This has led to an opening up of the language of train stations. In the past it was the head building and shed. The station was built for the train, not the passengers. In the past it was a purely functional and sometimes temporary building in U.S. cities, or a replica of the airport experience in other places. Today, architects are designing much more significant buildings and adopt different approaches to solving the components of ticketing, waiting, shopping, transfer between modes of transportation, and so on. The key word of the day is "seamless journey." While no journey can be entirely seamless, the concept that planning, architecture, and design can contribute to making the travel experience more efficient is welcome. It also recognizes that a trip does not begin when a

passenger boards a train, but rather when the traveler leaves home or the point of origin of the trip. The station as a link in the chain of events of a journey is a significant change that has occurred recently. A review of the stations featured in the following pages shows that while some architects still seek to incorporate traditional components, such as a vaulted shed or clock tower, many are using train stations to explore issues common to many types of building. They are investigating avenues of research that extend beyond typology to issues of urban structure and the contribution of stations to the overall metropolitan milieu.

Another trend seen in some examples of current station building is a recuperation of the expression of the structure and an emphasis on the role of engineering in the art of building. Architect and engineer Santiago Calatrava makes the most dramatic gestures in this field. His Lyon-Satolas Station in France is a giant birdlike structure with a glass concourse that rests in only three places. The low concrete train shed is 500 meters long and is created by 53-meter-wide vaults of slender ribs supported by buttresses. Each element is visible and identifiable. Engineering becomes sculpture. This kind of celebration of engineering is also present in the work of many other architects, from Paul Andreu at the TGV station at Charles De Gaulle Airport in Roissy, northeast of Paris, to Nicholas Grimshaw at Waterloo, to Norman Foster in Hong Kong.

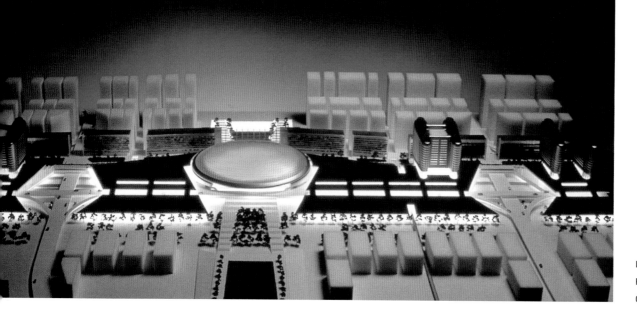

Whereas stations in the past may have been more sensitive to solving their functional requirements or reflecting, through their architecture, their mission as a transport center, today there is greater sensitivity to the role of the station in its context. In the case of the Channel Tunnel Terminal at Folkestone (see pp. 136–37) and Arbois TGV Station at Aix-en-Provence (see pp. 70–71), the architects have sought to integrate the stations within the natural landscape. Although the architectural language and the scope of the programs varies between the two stations, the idea of keeping the building low to the ground and surrounding it by extensively landscaped areas is common. Both Sandvika Station (see pp. 118–19) and Sleppenden Station (1993; see p. 23) in Norway by Arne Hendriksen are contextual without being mimetic. The concrete cylindrical structure of Sleppenden

Station is the "fortress" next to the stone wall. Wooden components are used extensively and support the wooden roof for the cylinder and the platforms. Hendriksen himself has said, "The tree is likely one of our great sources of inspiration."[5]

A rebirth of the architecture of rail stations is certainly under way in Europe. Japan, which relies heavily on public transportation and considers it a top priority, is also expanding its vocabulary and goals of station architecture, often encompassing the rail service within a multipurpose building. Certain countries in Southeast Asia, especially those that are experiencing rapid economic growth, are increasingly using transport networks, and subsequently the transport station, as an important component in urban and regional planning. The station as the focal point for new towns and settlements is increasingly common. It is the U.S.A. that still sorely lags behind, although there are some rays of hope, first seen in the restoration of historic monuments and now in some attempts to building significant station buildings.

The challenges facing the future lie not only in the architecture of stations, but also in the political and economic spheres. The multifaceted goal of railway companies must seek a redefinition of rail travel. It must not be seen as the mode of transport for those unable to afford a private car or airplane ticket. It needs to be part of a network, serving certain routes that trains can do best, namely commuter traffic, longer trips of up to 400 kilometers, and even longer-

Sleppenden Station, Norway,
Arne Henriksen

distance travel for those who prefer to take the time to stay close to the ground. Train travel certainly provides ecological incentives to make it the mode of choice, particularly because traveling by train uses proportionally less energy per person than private cars or airplanes. Quality architecture for rail travel can certainly contribute to the goal. Stations that express the importance of rail travel through high-quality design and lasting and beautiful materials certainly reflect the value we place on this mode of travel. Stations that create a focal center and gathering place, rather than introducing an infrastructural divide within a city, can contribute to—and indeed elevate—the quality of life of an area.

Without a doubt, the issues facing contemporary architects in any type of building also confront those who undertake the design of train stations. In addition to the more ordinary challenges station architecture must deal with, however, the particular demands of transportation—its intensity of use, its strenuous requirements of accommodating trains themselves as well as their passengers—make this form of architecture more demanding than others. Nevertheless, we can expect to see an even richer variety of approaches in the future, if, of course, station architects are given the opportunity, budget, and support necessary to tackle such an important task.

1 John Ruskin, *The Seven Lamps of Architecture*, in E.T. Cook and Alexander Wedderburn (eds.), *The Works of John Ruskin*, vol. VIII, p. 159. (*The Seven Lamps of Architecture* was originally published in 1849.)

2 Carroll L.V. Meeks, *The Railroad Station: An Architectural History* [1956], New York (Dover) 1995, p. ix.

3 Jack W. Seto, *Railroad Stations in the U.S.*, Council of Planning Librarians Exchange Bibliography #1450, Monticello IL, 1978, p. 1.

4 See Marcus Binney and David Pearce, *Railway Architecture*, London (Orbis Publishing) 1979, for an analysis of historic buildings and the potential for reuse, and Peter Burman and Michael Stratton (eds.), *Conserving the Railway Heritage*, London (E & FN Spon) 1997.

5 *Arkitekturhefte 1*, booklet published on the occasion of the Timber awards granted on behalf of the Council for Wood Information, by Arne Hendriksen and Christian Norberg-Schultz, 1998, p. 9.

DESIGNING FOR THEIR NEEDS:
PASSENGER TRAINS FOR TODAY AND TOMORROW
IN EUROPE, JAPAN, AND NORTH AMERICA

CLAUDIA WESSNER

Pennsylvania Station Redevelopment
Project, Skidmore, Owings & Merrill LLP,
computer rendering of platform area

The railroad train is a highly evolved mass-transportation system that still holds its place in the worldwide travel market. In the past, the train and its operating system were often developed and manufactured for a single, specific application; nowadays, new designs increasingly resemble one another. One reason for this is that increased mobility has made the world "a smaller place" and increased the frequency of exchanges; another is the increasing degree of contact between formerly separate transportation networks. Companies with global operations and long experience of railroad engineering are building train sets for operating organizations in different countries and continents. Established standards and norms make the manufacture, operation, and maintenance of trains easier and more economic. Nevertheless, before a train actually runs, a long development process is necessary, and industrial design ought ideally to be involved in this from an early stage. Such is the complexity of the process that the industrial designer must work closely, both as a generalist and as a specialist, with experts in a wide variety of other disciplines.

Nowadays, the design and development of a railroad vehicle takes only three years, although a further one and a half years may be needed to adapt the product to the client's specific needs. In developing a new train, the design process follows a classic product-development pattern, as follows:

- Analysis of start position
- Definition of objectives
- Concept phase
- Feasibility study
- Finalization of the design
- Detailing
- Documentation of design process
- Design support for subsequent processes

The initial analysis comprises a study of lifestyle and cultural factors, the usage that the train will receive, and the shortcomings of equipment previously used. At the next stage, all relevant objectives are defined with reference to legal, cultural, and technical requirements. This is followed by a stage when the first concept sketches are made. These include outlines of working sequences, as well as ideas for the external shape of the vehicle, the layout of interior fittings, and the choice of materials. Research into products already on the market is an integral part of the design process. No design ever starts completely from scratch, and the best use is made of existing components. Once the available concepts have been narrowed down, there follows the practical design process, in which—for example—internal layouts are worked out and lighting concepts established.

To evaluate the designs, a digital mockup is made. For difficult spatial problems it may at times be necessary to make a full-size physical mockup, usually of a single car. For high-speed trains, models are tested in a wind tunnel to optimize the aerodynamic properties of the design. Finally, all components are worked out in detail, in both two and three dimensions. Design support is maintained during the production process, for example by checking color matches. The client company must be closely involved throughout, to make sure that its wishes and suggestions are fully taken into account.

The intended use of the vehicle, its target customer group, and the intended location affect the emphases and requirements that govern the designers' work. For example, a train for a regional network needs to have considerably more doors and more standing room than a high-speed train. Such aspects as journey time, frequency, and ticket prices, as well as service and a pleasant, comfortable, and safe travel experience, are also vital to the train's eventual customer appeal.

High-Speed Trains

One way in which train travel can be made more attractive is by cutting journey times. This is the province of the high-speed train. At present, seventeen countries possess high-speed train

12X locomotive, wind-tunnel test

ICE 3, exterior of mock-up

ICE 3, bistro car

ICE 3, front lounge

systems. In the competition among different transportation systems, high-speed trains are a vital lifeline for railroad companies. Train travel becomes competitive on a journey of between 100 and 600 kilometers from city center to city center. If we include travel to and from stations at either end, the train is quicker than the plane or the car; it is also statistically more reliable, more energy-efficient, more comfortable, and in some respects safer. At the same time, it has become evident that high speed in itself is not enough. The level of comfort needs to be higher than in an airplane for an equal journey time: an insight that is reflected in a number of high-speed train operations.

One of the latest high-speed trains is the German ICE 3. As a successor to the ICE and ICE 2, which set international standards for rail travel, this went into service with the national carrier, Deutsche Bahn (DB), on the occasion of Expo 2000 in Hanover. Exterior and interior design is by Neumeister Design of Munich, under the direction of one of the world's most distinguished train designers, Alexander Neumeister. In some respects, the ICE 3 harks back to its predecessors, which were also designed by Neumeister. The exterior has an iconic clarity, elegance, and dynamism. The distinctive strip window, punctuated by oval panes in the doors, was an innovatory feature of the first ICE. In ICE 3 the strip continues to the nose of the head car and gives visual expression to the changed structure of

the train, in which the whole motive power system has been moved from the two end cars to the underside. ICE 3 has no power car, so that more of the interior is now available for passengers' use, and there is more seating. The train operator is separated from passengers only by a glass screen. This glazing allows passengers to see the track ahead, through the cab, and to enjoy the sensation of traveling at 330 kph. The clear glass can be converted into frosted glass at a moment's notice. In formal terms, the ICE 3's design incorporates elements of both train and air travel. The proportions of the train's elongated, aerodynamic nose are a visual expression of speed.

The train is composed of two end cars and six intermediate cars, with seating for 415 passengers in all. Two trains can readily be coupled together. The interior has been redesigned for added comfort, while at the same time the number of seats has increased. Internal fittings are attuned to the needs of business travelers: there are public telephones, power sockets for laptops, a mailbox, and a fax machine. More than 30% of the accommodation is in first-class seats, in a 1+2 arrangement. First-class cars are wood-paneled, with classic elegance, and the seats are dark-blue leather. Seats located directly behind another seat have video screens. There are also a number of compartments with four or five seats for use as conference rooms, equipped with telephones and separated from the rest of the car by glass screens. In second class the seats are

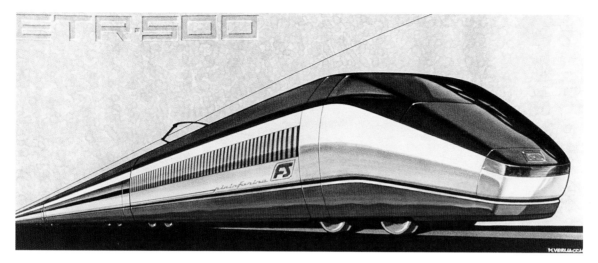

ETR 500, one-system locomotive

arranged one behind the other, in an open-plan car with a 2+2 layout, interspersed with a number of seats grouped to face one another across tables.

The generous and convincingly clear design relies on high-quality materials and harmonious color, and is supported by sensitive detailing. Facilities such as an onboard shop, special family compartments, and headphones at every seat reflect a concern for the individuality of the traveler. The outcome of the design process carries total conviction, thanks to the early involvement of the design team in the development process and its subsequent close collaboration with DB. The ICE 3 has set new standards for quality in railroad travel, not only in Germany but internationally. Thirteen of the fifty trains on order have been built with modular add-ons, as multisystem units for cross-border operation. Built by Siemens and Adtranz, this version of the ICE 3 is currently one of the most advanced trains in service anywhere in the world.

The possibility of a new model, the ICE 4, is still under discussion. With increased width and a 2+3 seating layout, an additional 180 seats could be created within the same overall length. In contrast to the ICE 3, which has a design profile somewhere between that of a train and that of an airplane, the ETR500, which went into operation in 1996 with the Italian state railroad, FS (Ferrovie dello Stato), is consciously designed with reference to its product identity as a railroad train. The first two experimental

train sets, under the name of ETRY500, operated on the route between Florence and Rome in 1990–92. The timeless rigor and simplicity of the exterior design is emphasized by the color scheme, in which graphic continuity is the predominant element. Dark colors outline the form, emphasize the ends of the train, mask those areas where dirt accumulates, and optically conceal ventilation slits.

The interior design of the experimental trains was inspired by that of a passenger aircraft, both in its materials and in such typical elements as closed overhead baggage racks. Decor elements were integrated with the overall effect of the interior; their simplicity and strong formal emphasis were extremely novel for the period. When the ETR500 went into series production with Trevi Consortium, the exterior design of the prototype was retained, but the interior was changed. The "airliner style" was abandoned in favor of a warmer welcome for passengers boarding the train. An increased use of textiles and glass made the internal space visually larger. To avoid the monotony created by the use of a restricted range of materials (as in the prototype), varied upholstery patterns are used to create strong contrasts. The sumptuous, rounded forms and gleaming wall coverings of the bistro car create the same effect.

The first thirty train sets were designed for the Italian domestic rail network. For the requirements of the emergent European high-speed railroad

Acela Express, exterior,
computer-generated image

system, the remaining thirty train sets were built with multivoltage power cars. These went into service in 1998. The power car and train operator's cab are designed for use on both the Italian and French railroad systems. The nose of the train was also modified and rounded to improve its aerodynamics. The new design was created and wind-tunnel-tested by the Italian design consultancy Pininfarina. Individual elliptical lamps, a flat, one-piece windscreen, and a new color scheme emphasized the design change. At a speed of 300 kph, the ETR 500 carries a maximum load of 700 passengers between principal cities all over Italy.

The Acela Express, which went into service with Amtrak at the end of 2000, is the first high-speed train in the U.S.A. On the strength of a financing package and its experience in North American railcar construction, the Canadian-based Bombardier Transportation secured the contract to build twenty high-speed train sets in conjunction with GEC Alstom. The bogies and traction units are from the French TGV (Train à Grande Vitesse, or high-speed train), made by Alstom. The TGV has also influenced the design of the head car.

The Acela Express runs between Boston and Washington D.C., through the most densely populated area of the U.S.A. Despite the use of existing track, with frequent curves, a maximum speed of 240 kph and the use of tilting-train technology enable it to cut the journey time by forty-five minutes. To establish a

market presence, Amtrak engaged the branding consultancy Ideo, which developed the Acela brand as the emblem of a new kind of rail travel. The blue of the trademark is carried through the interior and exterior design of the train. With one first-class car, four business-class cars, and one dining car, the Acela Express is designed with business travelers in mind. The 304 passengers have access to telephones, fax, video and audio entertainment, and power outlets for laptops. Seat groups can be reserved for business meetings. Typical features of American rail travel are the footrests and the swivel seats. The interior, an in-house design by Amtrak, is based on that of a passenger aircraft. The enclosed, airline-style baggage racks emphasize the narrowing of the space toward the top (a consequence of the tilting-train technology), with the result that the cross-section of the interior resembles that of an airliner. In first class, meals are prepared in two curtained-off galleys at the ends of the car, as in an airplane, and served to passengers in their seats.

As a result of U.S. safety requirements, which are more exacting than those in Europe, all the seats are anchored to the floor, every window incorporates an emergency exit, and the forms of the interior detailing are rounded. The Acela Express is the first train to meet the Federal Railroad Administration's Tier II Crashworthiness Standard, and has been described as the train least liable to malfunction of any in the world. This gives it a weight disadvantage

JR 500, head car

in relation to other high-speed trains: it is 45% heavier than the comparable TGV. In densely populated areas there are stretches of unfenced track, on which debris is frequently encountered; consequently, all underfloor components require added protection.

In Japan, the birthplace of high-speed rail travel, conditions for high-speed train operation are very different. The country's high population density creates heavy traffic, for which railroads successfully compete against other modes of transportation. Speed, frequency, and punctuality are the main factors that enable the railroads to maintain this market dominance. The railroads were privatized in 1985 and divided among six privately owned commercial operations.

The Shinkansen demonstrates the competitiveness and effectiveness of rail for communication between major cities. The railroads enjoy a considerable advantage over air travel for all journeys of 600 kilometers or less. On the Tokyo–Yamagata route, for example, their market share is 88%. The fastest Shinkansen trains run mainly on dedicated tracks, to avoid delays created by slower traffic. An example is the route between Osaka and Tokyo. In 1998, a total of 368,000 passengers used the line every day. In spite of bad weather and earthquakes, the average deviation from the schedule was approximately thirty-six seconds per trip.

The JR 500, with a running speed of 300 kph and a maximum speed of 320 kph, is one of the fastest trains in the world. Since 1997, it has been in operation on JR West's Osaka-Fukuoka route, where its main competitor is air travel. The exterior design of the JR 500 was developed from an earlier study by Neumeister Design for the HST 350. The principal manufacturer, Kawasaki Heavy Industries, used this as the basis to optimize the design of the head car. The train received the 1998 Brunel Award, an international prize recognizing quality design in railway architecture and locomotive and car design.

The interior looks traditional. Both in green (first) and standard class, the seats are arranged one behind the other in an open plan. This rigid arrangement, with no grouping or large tables, creates a uniform spatial impression reminiscent of a bus or airplane. The only space to which the individual passenger can withdraw—in order to breastfeed, for example—is a single, small, multipurpose compartment. The sidewalls of the car are curved, in order to maximize internal space and minimize interaction with oncoming trains, and this reinforces the look of an aircraft interior. To increase stability and economize on weight, the walls consist of an aluminum honeycomb structure between inner and outer skins. Although the cellular cross-section, seating arrangement, and fold-down tables are reminiscent of a passenger-aircraft interior, this resemblance is incidental to the designer's main intention, which is to optimize the functioning of the train when carrying large numbers of passengers. This concern is evident in the clean lines and the sense of openness but also in the seating layout: 2+2 in first class and 3+2 in second. Each second-class car is built to accommodate 100 passengers, and the whole sixteen-car train set has 1324 seats, of which only 15% are first class.

Heavy trains traveling at high speeds create numerous problems, one of which is that of powerful pressure waves. The dramatic shape of the nose, like a bird's beak, 15 meters long, creates a streamlined profile that minimizes pressure waves both at tunnel entrances and in encounters with oncoming trains. The taper of the head car is such that the area of its cross-section increases in approximately linear progression toward the rear. As a result, this car is 2 meters longer than the others. Similarly, in the design of the striking nose unit of the Talgo 350, which, with its operating speed of 350 kph, will be the fastest train in Europe, a salient design factor was the linear increase in cross-section from nose to first passenger car. The power unit was jointly developed by the Spanish company Talgo and Adtranz, with support from the Munich design consultancy Haslacher. The train—provisionally equipped with Talgo "Seventh Generation" passenger cars— is currently under test as part of a competition organized by the Spanish national railroad company, Renfe, for the Madrid–Barcelona route.

Tilting-Train Technology

The demand for fast travel is rapidly increasing. Although nations and governments frequently opt for high-speed trains in order to prove the modernity of their transportation policies, existing route networks are often unsuited for high-speed operation; nor is open, flat terrain always available for the building of new, straight tracks, as it was in the case of the TGV network in France. High costs and environmental concerns have led to the search for other ways of reducing journey times. Tilting-train technology was developed as an alternative to building new routes and straightening old ones.

Tilting trains can attain high speeds without the need for heavy braking, even on tracks with frequent bends. On curved sections of track they are automatically tilted to a maximum of 8 degrees by hydraulic and electromechanical tilting systems, lessening the centrifugal force that acts on the passengers as the train negotiates bends. With minimal modifications, trains can thus be operated on existing tracks at speeds up to one-third faster. The cost of re-equipping for tilting-train technology is only one-tenth of that of building a high-speed train and new tracks.

In Italy, Fiat Ferroviaria developed the Pendolino, a tilting train with an important place in railroad history. The prototype first ran on a test track in 1971. Pendolino trains now travel at speeds 30% higher than conventional trains and are used to cross the

Amtrak Cascades, bistro car

Amtrak Cascades, first-class interior

Alps. The Pendolino's active tilting technology is currently used in some 70% of all tilting trains worldwide. With low environmental impact and investment costs, the result was a new kind of train travel, more comfortable for the passengers and considerably more punctual.

The Pendolino ETR 460 is the ancestor of all new high-speed trains. First put into service by FS in 1993, it is used to work a number of lines in Italy at a maximum speed of 250 kph. Unlike its predecessors, this electric-powered multiple unit has the tilting system beneath the floor; this frees up the whole space in the passenger cell.

Exterior and interior design are by Giugiaro and are pleasingly uncluttered. Colors and materials, unlike those on the ETR 500, are restrained and neutral. The interior components, with their mostly straight lines, are primarily made from plastics. Glass appears hardly at all, and the use of textiles has been very much reduced. Styling of some interior components—notably the bar in the bistro car—recalls that of the ETR 500. The Pendolino ETR 460, the first tilting train to possess a restaurant car, is available in a number of versions. The one with telephones, video screens, and laptop power outlets is very little different from the latest high-speed trains. The versatile Pendolino is currently used in Germany, Finland, Switzerland, Spain, Portugal, and the Czech Republic.

In the passive tilting system developed by Talgo in Spain, the car frame is suspended from a point above the center of gravity, so that on a curve it swings like a pendulum. This system was introduced in Spain in 1980 and at present is in use in Canada, France, Italy, Portugal, Switzerland, and the U.S.A. The Talgo system is used by the Amtrak Cascades, which has been in operation in the Cascadia Corridor, between Vancouver, British Columbia, and Eugene, Oregon, since 1999. The exterior of the Cascades train, designed for Amtrak by Cesar Vergara, is especially distinctive. The height difference between the American F59 diesel locomotive and the markedly lower Spanish passenger cars is spanned by curved fins that extend for part of the length of the baggage car. The transition is further emphasized by a "wave" graphic.

The use of single-axle bogies means that the cars are short, and consequently the unit has more than twice as many exits as a traditional passenger train. With a speed of 200 kph, this lightweight train has 268 seats and is aimed mainly at business travelers. The interior design is often described as European-looking. Adjustable seats with individual reading lamps, video and audio entertainment in every seat, folding tables, and power outlets for laptops afford perfect working conditions. A telephone is provided on the train. First and second class are distinguished only by the seating layout (2+1 as against 2+2) and a slightly different choice of decor materials. Large windows (a typically European feature), varied use of materials, and recurrent patterning are reminders of the importance of the train's visual image both to passengers and owners; as are the map of the Pacific Northwest on the ceiling of the bistro car, with the route picked out in lights, and the reflective stainless-steel external surfaces with matte strips. With bicycle racks provided in the baggage car, this train is open to a variety of users.

Europe

The process of cultural globalization—clearly visible in the design of the Amtrak Cascades—is most marked in Europe, with its densely populated areas and its moves toward political union. Territories that once were entirely separate are now becoming economically integrated and consequently demand upgraded transportation links. Cross-border rail traffic raises a number of technical and organizational problems. These include different operating voltages, gauges, signaling systems, languages, corporate identities, and even ticket-sales methods. Such problems pose new demands for the next generation of trains, already under development. The German and French rail chiefs have already agreed that the next generation of high-speed trains will be jointly developed. A European Union project is under way to develop a single standard cab, thus easing the train operator's work and improving travel safety. The purpose is to harmonize cross-border operation.

The first of the new trains designed for international operation is the Eurostar. When it first

Eurostar, bistro car

Eurostar, second-class interior

Eurostar, exterior

went into operation in 1994, this was regarded as the most complex and advanced train to date. Running through three countries and the Channel Tunnel, the Eurostar connects three capital cities: London, Paris, and Brussels. Eurostar was developed as a joint project by the three national rail operators of France, Great Britain, and Belgium, SNCF, Eurostar (UK), and SNCB, who own, respectively, sixteen, eleven, and four trains.

To this end, the International Project Group was set up by all three governments in 1987. In the course of development, surprising differences emerged not only in the railroad operations of the three nations but also in national tastes. Based on TGV technology, the Eurostar is designed to operate within the three different national networks. It has different overhead power collection systems for Belgium and France, and in Britain it takes current from a third rail. Signal systems, too, change in the course of each journey. Because British station platforms are higher, the original TGV passenger shell design had to be modified.

The production train sets were manufactured by a consortium of British, Belgian, and French companies, under the leadership of GEC Alstom. Industrial design, too, was shared among a number of consultancies. Jones Garrard of London designed the head car, which won a Design & Art Direction Silver Award for outstanding product design in industry and transportation. Design of passenger areas was by the French designer Roger Tallon, who

already had years of experience with TGV trains. The Belgian firm of Inov designed entrance areas and restrooms. Tallon's design for the bar was rejected, and instead the British firm Tilney Lumsden Shane was called in. This division of responsibility has led to formal inconsistencies between the aerodynamic shape of the nose, the TGV-style design of the passenger areas, and the look of the bistro car.

In addition to the exigencies of cross-border operation, this 300 kph train—which, with its 18 cars and 794 seats, carries almost as many passengers as two Boeing 747 jets—has to meet the specific safety requirements that arise from the use of the Channel Tunnel. For safety reasons, the train is designed to be automatically divided in half within two minutes, as soon as the passengers in one half have been evacuated to the other. The two power cars can be uncoupled from the rest of the train in the same way. In case of power failure, compatible couplings enable the train to be hauled out of the tunnel by diesel-electric locomotives. For ease of operation, the computers and other equipment in the cabs function in three languages. Crews are trained to work in three languages, and public announcements on the train are given in two, three, or four languages, always starting with the language of the country through which the train is traveling.

In Spain, the problem of different gauges in cross-border operation has found a solution in the design of the Talgo XXI. First supplied to Renfe in

TGV Duplex

TGV Duplex, first-class interior

1999, this diesel-powered express, which travels at 220 kph, is one of the first of its kind to be equipped with an adjustable wheel action. The train passes through a gauge-conversion point in which the gauge of the bogies can be changed from 1435 mm to 1668 mm. At a speed of 15 kph, the whole train is converted without human intervention in just one minute. The distinctive design of the head car, with its gentle profile, pleasing proportions, aerodynamic shape, and flowing contours, is by Neumeister Design. Unlike the tilting passenger cars of the Talgo Seventh Generation series, the diesel-power car of this train has no tilt function. A power car for dual-system electric operation, with passive tilting technology, is under development in a joint venture with Adtranz.

Quantity and High Speed

Further important considerations in train design are economy of operation and passenger capacity. On busy routes, often every seat counts. The busiest high-speed route in France, between Paris and Lyon, was running to full capacity shortly after its opening in 1981. Attempts to solve the problem by coupling two train sets together proved inadequate and required longer station platforms. This led to the development of a bi-level high-speed train, the TGV Duplex, which went into service with SNCF in 1996. This, the third generation of the TGV family, is manufactured by GEC Alstom. Despite the extra

height, it travels at 300 kph. Equal in mass to a conventional TGV, and with the same operating parameters, the Duplex can carry 45% more passengers without additional crew members. As with the ICE, use of an extruded-aluminum construction for the body shell yields a 20% saving in weight. Improved aerodynamics and tighter connections between cars mean that wind resistance is only 4% higher than that of a single-deck TGV.

With a length of 200 meters, the train set, with eight passenger cars and a power car at each end, can carry 545 passengers. Two trains can be coupled together to increase capacity to 1100. Despite these high passenger loads, comfort was a major design objective, and the train set accordingly includes a 36% proportion of first-class seats.

The design of the TGV Duplex is by Roger Tallon; it received the Brunel Award for Rolling Stock/Long Distance Passenger Trains at the 1996 award ceremony in Copenhagen. The clean lines of the exterior design, with its aerodynamic nose and well-balanced proportions, are carried through in the design of passenger spaces. Communication between cars is on the upper deck, as are the restrooms, so that passenger flow is kept on this level. Top-deck passengers need use the stairs only on boarding and leaving the train, and the lower-deck compartments are largely undisturbed. The upper level mostly consists of open-plan cars; the seating layout is varied by the inclusion of tables, additional baggage

Shinkansen E4 Series, double deck

areas, and glass screens. With business compartments, family compartments, and children's play corners, the lower deck is more attuned to passengers' individual requirements. The interiors are largely lined with gray felt, primarily for reasons of sound insulation. The expanse of gray is relieved by colored inserts in the ceilings and lively, striped upholstery fabrics; in first class these extend to the armrests. The background lighting and the downward-directed reading lamps in the baggage racks are configured in such a way that the ceiling remains unlit, thus making the space look larger than it is. The disadvantage here is that the baggage racks themselves are unlit. The same effect is used in the bistro car, which is on the upper deck.

Similar requirements, arising from high levels of passenger usage, are found in Japan. An extreme case is the rush-hour commuter traffic created by the drift to the suburbs in the Tokyo area. The Tohoku Shinkansen route is a case in point. Here, increasing efforts have been made to meet the capacity problem by taking over dedicated freight tracks and by increasing speeds. For this route, and for the Joetsu Line, another bi-level train has been developed: the Shinkansen Max E4. Since 1997 this has been in operation with JR East, the largest Japanese railroad company, with the highest passenger usage rates of any system in the world. With a maximum speed of 240 kph, an eight-car train set with a power car at each end can carry 817 passengers. A train

consisting of two multiple units coupled together, with a seating capacity of 1634 and a total length of 400 meters, carries more seated passengers than any other high-speed train in the world. This high passenger capacity is achieved in the standard-class accommodation that fills most of the train by a seating layout that accommodates five seats per row. Third class has 20% of the seats, arranged 3+3. Only 6% of the seats belong to green, or first, class, with a 2+2 seating layout.

As with the JR 500, the whole train is made up of open-plan cells, with seats facing the direction of travel. This is made possible because the seats can be rotated through 180 degrees. The three classes are distinguished only by a few functions. Green class has wider seats, individual reading lamps, leg rests, and different lighting fixtures from standard class. In third class, which contains the unreserved accommodation, individual seats are replaced by fixed bench seats with only two armrests for each. There are four different restroom types, used separately by men and women. The whole train has just one small sales point and no on-board entertainment. Its advantage lies in its high speed, frequency, and ticket availability at short notice.

Exterior design is by the TDO design consultancy. The head car design bears a distinct resemblance to that of the E2, also operated by JR East, and to the Series 700 of JR Central, both of which also feature a transition from a rounded to a highly angular cross-

Crusaris Regina, exterior

Crusaris Regina, elevator

section. The aerodynamic nose helps to minimize pressure waves. The organic headlamp form emphasizes the flowing lines.

Other Requirements

Economy and flexibility were all-important factors in the development of the Flexliner, a design originated by the Danish company ABB. Basic modules, each made up of two cars, can be coupled together at their vertical ends with a distinctive air-filled rubber front and automatic coupling. Coupling and decoupling are controlled by the train operator and can be completed within one minute. The cab doors and driving positions swing away to one side, yielding a train with perfect end-to-end communication. Units with different forms of motive power can operate as parts of the same train. This not only means a high degree of flexibility and economy for the operating organization, which can schedule trains to divide *en route*, but often enables the passenger to avoid a change. Versions of the Flexliner, built by Adtranz and tried and tested in use over the past ten years, are now operating in seven countries.

The latest multiple-unit design to incorporate the Flexliner nose is the Öresund train, CRUSARIS Contessa, which runs between Copenhagen and Malmö in Sweden. This entered service in 2000 and has a maximum speed of 180 kph. Its three cars carry 237 passengers. The design is a collaboration between Eleven Danes in Denmark and Adtranz

Sweden. It was awarded the Danish Design Prize for 2000. As with the original Flexliner, the exterior design is strongly practical, plain, and succinct. The clean, bright, functional interior is harmoniously conceived in every detail and offers an exemplary instance of designing created to last. For example, the graphic elements that relieve the plainness of the wall panels reappear in the glass screens and in the baggage compartments.

Nordic Comfort

Other considerations apply to the design of the Swedish regional and interregional train, CRUSARIS Regina. Adtranz developed the Regina for the Scandinavian market in the absence of a firm client order, using the CRUSARIS product platform as a base. The Adtranz Sweden Industrial Center was involved in the development process from an early stage. The design platform has a modular capability that makes it readily adaptable to the needs of specific operating organizations. The pursuit of economy combined with comfort is notably visible in the width of the car, which allows 25% more seats than comparable trains with an equal level of comfort.

Reflecting Scandinavian classlessness and social cohesion, the CRUSARIS Regina has single-class accommodation and special features for disabled access. The elevator built into the entrance and circulation area bypasses two steps and can be used while the train is in motion. Its controls are easily accessible, so that disabled passengers can enter and leave the train without assistance. Even while the elevator is in use, other passengers can pass without obstruction. The exterior and interior design are clearly structured. Open-plan passenger compartments, made more spacious by the generous width of the car, are fitted out plainly but to a high-quality standard. This shows itself in the harmonious choice of materials. Muted colors combine with stainless steel, oxidized aluminum, native beech wood, and textiles specially designed and made for the train. For all its comfort, the train is designed for a high level of passenger usage, and this is reflected in its low-maintenance surfaces, linoleum flooring,

and provision of additional folding seats in lobby areas. The CRUSARIS Regina, with a top speed of 200 kph, entered service in 2000. It has since been ordered by a number of operators and has received the prize for Excellent Swedish Design 2000.

Luxury and High-Altitude Applications

A marked contrast is offered by the Crystal Panoramic Express, operated since 1993 by the Montreux-Oberland-Bernois railroad (MOB). The train operates between Montreux and Lenk in Switzerland; with comparatively few seats, it caters for a select clientele of international winter-sport visitors, for whom it seeks to provide a quality experience. Design is by Pininfarina. Each end car

Chrystal Panoramic Express

Gardermoen Airport Shuttle, interior

Gardermoen Airport Shuttle, exterior

is furnished as an observation car throughout, with open groups of seating. The windows extend upward over the edges of the ceiling; to give passengers a view forward, the train operator's position has been raised to roof level. As seen from outside, this raised section emphasizes the two ends of the train. In the interiors, with special racks and baggage compartments, sharp corners and exposed screws were avoided in order to protect winter-sport equipment and clothing. Special features necessitated by the maximum altitude of 2000 meters include frost-insulated water tanks and UV-filter glass.

Airport Rail Links

Airport shuttle systems present special requirements. They are primarily designed to cater to business travelers and for those with heavy baggage. The central design objective must be to provide a comfortable and trouble-free journey between the airport and downtown.

The Heathrow Express has been running between central London and Heathrow Airport since 1998; it is operated by Heathrow Express Ltd, a subsidiary of the British Airports Authority. Manufactured by Siemens Transportation Systems Germany, the Heathrow Express was designed by Triangle Design, of London. The exterior is characterized by a distinctive rounded front, and by the smoked glass in the windows. Painted silver-gray, the train stands out markedly

from the trains of other operators. Before operation began, parts of the front had to be painted yellow for added visibility, in accordance with the regulations of the track-operation company, Railtrack. Car entrances are on the same level as station platforms. The interior of each car, divided between first- and second-class accommodation, is made up of flexible, interchangeable components, and, with a modular system, it can be remodeled within eight hours. The seats face toward the nearest baggage compartment, so that passengers can keep an eye on their own belongings. Despite a short journey time of fifteen minutes, there are public telephones on the train. Each car has four video screens displaying airport information. The interiors are enlivened by the use of light as a design element and of varied but related colors for the seat covers. Damaged seats can be taken out and replaced with ease.

In Norway, the Airport Shuttle between Oslo and Gardermoen Airport was the country's first high-speed rail link. Built by Adtranz Sweden, the train went into operation with NSB Gardermobanan A/S in 1998; its design is by the Oslo design consultancy Meyer, directed by Terje Meyer. The striking exterior, streamlined and powerful-looking, has a raised cockpit windscreen that gives the nose something of the appearance of a jumbo jet. The monochrome, silver-gray color scheme accentuates this effect. The distinctive feature of the middle car is a continuous window strip.

The interior design concentrates on the train's specific function. The doors are displaced from the ends toward the center of each car, and each gives access to a single compartment on either side. This ensures an equally short walk to all seats and a smooth flow of passengers into and out of the car. A central baggage rack in the entrance area and two more at the entrance to each seating compartment minimize movement of heavy baggage. The upper part of the central baggage unit contains video screens for airport information. All the seats face toward the entrances, so that passengers have a constant view of the entrance, their own baggage, and the screens. The train is functional, plain, and extremely comfortable. A high power-to-weight ratio and a maximum speed of 210 kph are necessary in order to cover the distance of 48 kilometers, with a difference in altitude of 200 meters, in the specified time of nineteen minutes.

Future Prospects

Despite a large number of new developments, the basic technical concept of railroad transportation has not changed. With conventional trains, any large increase in operating speeds creates a series of problems, including instability, noise pollution, and wear between wheels and track. The development of maglev (magnetic levitation) technology marks a considerable advance, since – although a track is still required – the wheel-rail interface is eliminated.

A linear drive motor and friction-free operation make possible higher speeds, minimal wear and tear, and improved passenger comfort. Noise is almost entirely eliminated, with the exception of the slipstream. One disadvantage is that there is no existing track network; entirely new lines have to be built.

The German and Japanese governments have invested billions in research and development for maglev technology. Now, after more than three decades of tests and development, commercial operation is just around the corner. Since 1997, two Superconducting Maglev Test Vehicles have been running on the Yamanashi Maglev Test Line in Japan to determine speed and noise levels, reliability, and cost in regular operation. In 1999 the line set a speed record of 552 kph. The trains will be operated by JR Central on the Tokyo–Osaka route.These maglev trains are propelled by an electrodynamic system in which magnetic fields are generated by magnets cooled by liquid helium to minus 270 degrees Celsius. As magnetic power is generated only when the vehicle is in motion, wheels are necessary for low speeds.

The design reflects the nature of the vehicle's movement: a halfway house between land travel and flying. The track, or guideway, encloses the vehicle on both sides; the aerodynamic design of the train and its flowing lines produce a virtually perfect fit. Access to these trains will not be from open station platforms. After passing along a totally enclosed access path with built-in magnetic shields, passengers will enter the train thorough an upward-opening door. There is no driving position or cockpit at the head of the train. A small compartment in back of the first magnet bogie will contain a monitor giving a view of the tracks transmitted from a camera at the nose. There is a permanent communication link to the control room. The tiny windows, the seating layout, and the baggage lockers are strongly reminiscent of the interior of an airliner. A four-section train carries a maximum of 224 passengers.

In Germany, the Siemens/Thyssen/Adtranz consortium has built the Transrapid, a maglev train using a different propulsion system from the Japanese vehicle. This system has been approved for the first commercial maglev line in China. It is planned that in 2003 three units with a maximum speed of 500 kph will link Shanghai with Pudong International Airport. The Transrapid is propelled by a long-stator linear motor. The train's levitation system, which encloses the track, uses electromagnets. The propulsion system is installed in the guideway. Unlike the Japanese vehicle, the Transrapid can continue to hover while stationary, and therefore it has no wheels but only landing skids.

The exterior design of the prototype Transrapid 08 resembles that of the Transrapid 07, designed by Neumeister Design. Only the nose and color scheme have been changed. Although the classic strip windows resemble those of the ICE, the form of the unit follows function and therefore differs markedly from that of any conventional train. The nose is low, for aerodynamic reasons. The distinctive large, dark area at the front end contains the train operator's window.

The interior design of the prototype is by the Swiss design consultancy NOSE and was awarded the iF Product Design Award 2001. Functionality, openness, transparency, and a consistently high-tech style give visual expression to the sophistication of the technology and the unprecedented nature of the vehicle. The rectilinear motifs of the decorative trim reflect the theme of magnetic technology. The lighting is used to emphasize the functional distinctions between different areas of the train.

The Transrapid system consumes less energy than a conventional railroad for equivalent performance; it tackles gradients up to 10%, and negotiates smaller-radius curves than high-speed trains. With high speeds, added passenger comfort, and low wear and tear, maglev systems are well placed to meet the needs of transportation and the environment in the twenty-first century. There is plenty to look forward to.

DON PHILLIPS

A LAND OF PROMISE:
THE FUTURE OF TRAIN TRAVEL IN THE UNITED STATES

Transrapid, German maglev
experimental train

As the nineteenth century faded into history, the shape of twentieth-century transportation was already visible. A passenger train had traveled at more than 160 kph behind a steam locomotive that looked more like a tea kettle on big wheels, feeding a new American fascination with speed. Henry Ford put-putted around his garage in his first automobile, which he called a "quadricycle," in 1896. The world was abuzz with the excitement of air travel as the new century dawned; the question was, who would be the first to build an airship that could fly under its own power? Ships, of course, had plied the oceans for many centuries.

The technology of passenger trains, automobiles, airplanes, and ships changed remarkably in the twentieth century. But, while many of today's futurists and transportation planners are betting the same thing will happen in the twenty-first century, in 2101 there will still be trains, automobiles, airplanes, and ships. Just better ones. The passenger train is perhaps the most intriguing of all these forms of transportation. "The past is prologue" has become so familiar a phrase that often it means little. But in the case of the passenger train, there is broad agreement among rail historians and futurists that the history of the passenger train in the twentieth century makes a persuasive argument

that it will be around at the end of the twenty-first.

John Hankey, a historian, contends that almost everything that was present at the end of the twentieth century, in travel and other technical fields, such as electricity and plumbing, was an "elaboration" on what was around at the beginning of the century.[1] Only a handful of concepts were pure inventions of the twentieth century, he says. "What had not happened by 1900 was quantum physics and space travel." Only after the beginning of the twentieth century did the world "go inward toward the atom and outward toward the stars." Hankey said he could argue that automobiles and airplanes were merely an elaboration on the passenger train because they all represented the world's desire for mobility and speed. Those same desires will drive transportation throughout the twenty-first century, he believes. "People are still going to want to ride in comfortable tubes."

There was a time in the twentieth century when a lot of people thought that fantastic forms of travel envisioned by science fiction would become a reality. But what happened to the passenger train—and the reasons why it did not die in the twentieth century— suggest that it will survive and thrive.

The passenger train entered the twentieth century in rude health. There were small but feisty steam locomotives, wooden cars, sometimes foolhardy engineers, and steel wheels on steel rails. Steam locomotives grew larger and more complicated, passenger cars began to be made of steel instead of wood, and the passenger train criss-crossed the country. Railroad companies, flush with money from freight and passenger operations, rebuilt their lines into faster and more heavy-duty thoroughfares.[2] Signal systems were improved to allow higher speeds with greater safety. The Pennsylvania Railroad rebuilt and electrified its New York–Washington line in the late 1920s and early 1930s—and that is basically the same roadbed, bridges, and tunnels that Amtrak uses today as its high-speed Northeast Corridor.[3]

By the early 1940s, the automobile and the Great Depression had reduced the railroads' passenger loads. The outbreak of the Second World War, however, gave them a chance to show their mettle. They met a challenge that stretched them almost to breaking point, as they became part of freedom's supply line.[4] After the war, when traffic continued to fall, the railroads pretended the decline was only temporary and went on a buying binge for new diesel locomotives and sleek passenger cars. The word "streamliner'" entered the American lexicon.[5] But even speed, wonderful service, and new equipment could not hold enough passengers to make the passenger train economic. Passenger trains hauled 75% of all intercity passengers who used public

transport in 1944, near the end of the war.

By 1949, however, the railroads' share fell to 48%, then to 29% in 1960. The plunge was actually more acute than these numbers indicate because the car came into its own during that period, and millions of Americans were making use of the growing network of hard-surface highways. As the passenger rail service deteriorated and air travel became more commonplace, the passenger train entered a free-fall. Many railroads deliberately downgraded service to chase passengers away, and the only reason the trains did not disappear quickly was that the Interstate Commerce Commission (ICC). which regulated every aspect of the railroads, and state Public Service Commissions would not allow it.[6]

In 1958, an ICC official, Howard Hosmer, shocked the public with a report asserting that, if current trends continued, the sleeping car would be dead by 1965 and the passenger train itself would disappear by 1970.[7] The Hosmer report and its aftermath appears to have been the first shot in the battle to save the passenger train. By 1965, the passenger train—and all of railroading—had fallen on hard times. Passenger trains lost $421,000,000 that year, and it was becoming clear that the passenger deficit likely would drive major eastern freight railroads into bankruptcy.

The country faced a choice. Would it allow the passenger train to disappear from the American landscape? The answer was a resounding "no."

View of Metroliner for Anmtrak service
from Boston to Washington, D.C.

For reasons that may never be clear, there was something deep in the American subconscious that resonated to the sound of wheels on rails. In addition, something simple but amazing happened in the late 1960s that may have been the turning point in the future of the passenger train. Senator Claiborne Pell paid a visit to President Lyndon B. Johnson. Pell, a true believer in the passenger train, was the author of a hard-to-read but prophetic book called *Megalopolis Unbound.*[8] The purpose of Pell's visit was to persuade Johnson that he could carry the Northeast in the 1968 election if he would put the power of his office behind building a new fast train between Washington and New York.

Johnson was convinced. Using his legendary iron-fisted powers of persuasion, he dictated that a new fast train would be built before the election, and that it would run at 257 kph, then the speed of the Japanese Shinkansen. The Japanese would have nothing on the industrial might of the U.SA.

The Pennsylvania Railroad, which owned the track between Washington and New York, was anxious to curry favor with Johnson, and Chairman Stuart Saunders also ordered that considerable railroad resources be devoted to the new Metroliner project. In fact, the Pennsylvania—later renamed the Penn Central after its merger of February 1, 1968 with the New York Central—initially allocated $60,000,000 to the project, and the federal government provided $12,000,000.

The Metroliner did Johnson no good. He chose not to run for reelection rather than face the voters during the unpopular Vietnam War. And the self-propelled Metroliner cars themselves were a mechanical disaster. They reached 257 kph only during tests, and even at the lower 177 kph speed they rode like a cork on a windy pond. But the Metroliner was a resounding political and public-relations success after the first round-trip train pulled out of New York's Penn Station on January 16, 1969. In droves, the public ignored the rough ride and fought to get tickets on the first trains. Celebrities, especially Washington politicians, not only sang the Metroliner's praises but regularly rode it. The Metroliner became the symbol for rebirth of the passenger train, proof that Americans would ride trains if they were given good trains to ride. Meanwhile, the newspapers were filled with stories of passenger-train services being discontinued in the rest of the country. And the rest of the country began asking: if the Northeast can have the Metroliner, why can't we have something as good?

Congress heard the public enthusiasm and the public outcry, and on June 11, 1969, it began the great debate on what to do to save the passenger train—not whether to save the train. On that day, twenty-eight senators signed a resolution asking for a federal study on the best approach: either through subsidies or a government–industry corporation. Then, on July 16, the ICC recommended subsidies for passenger trains if railroads were to be forced to continue operating them. Intense debate raged inside Richard M. Nixon's administration about what to do, with various agencies fighting among themselves. Days stretched into months. Disgusted with the delay, Congress passed a bill setting up a semi-governmental corporation to run passenger trains. Initially it was called Railpax, borrowing the old telegraphers' term for passenger trains. Later, the name was changed to Amtrak.[9]

Nixon decided to sign the bill, apparently fearing that failure to do so would lead to nationwide bankruptcy in the railroad industry. That would mean nationalization of the railroads because no other means of transportation could efficiently haul coal, iron ore, grain, and the other bulk commodities of the economy to points that had no barge or ship access. Besides, people would never ride trains, or so thought the White House, so the new Amtrak would quickly disappear.

Amtrak took over most passenger trains on May 1, 1971. Unbelievably, people pushed aboard crowded, dirty, poorly maintained, and chronically late trains. And then they kept coming. A social decision was made by the public, and political decisions followed. Despite numerous efforts over the years by presidents of both parties to "zero-out" Amtrak's budget, Congress year after year restored the money. But Congress never gave Amtrak enough money to thrive, and the corporation bounced from crisis to crisis. If ever there was an argument that passenger trains will survive through the twenty-first century, it is that Amtrak has now survived for three decades in such a political climate.

But Amtrak's tale of survival masked other major political and societal changes that appear to have guaranteed the passenger train a more important role in the twenty-first century. First, all the other forms of transportation have become more crowded, and the public is tiring of this situation. Art shows us the mood of the public on transportation. According to Hankey, such movies as *Blade Runner* and *The Fifth Element* illustrate our pessimism about congestion and overcrowding of the transportation system, while *Star Trek* shows our fantasies for happier times.

With major airports at capacity, air service less reliable, and highways often parking lots in urban corridors, the very factor that appeared to be killing the passenger train now appears to be the major factor in securing its future.[10] Trip times by air and automobile are slowing just at the moment that short-distance passenger trains are gaining speed. By the end of the twentieth century, Amtrak's New York–Washington Northeast Corridor had already pulled far ahead of the two air shuttles. In New York–Washington "origin-and-destination" travel (not counting train passengers going to intermediate cities such as Philadelphia), Amtrak had 70% of the shuttle-like traffic and the two air shuttles split the other 30%.

William L. Withuhn, transportation curator of the Smithsonian Institution's Museum of American History, is a major proponent of the theory that speed is the most important factor in business travel, and that business-travel decisions will determine what forms of intercity transportation survive and prosper. The train was generally the business traveler's best option in much of the first half of the twentieth century, Withuhn said in a speech to the National Corridors Initiative in June 2000. He cited as a fine example 20th Century Limited's sixteen-hour overnight New York–Chicago schedule in 1938.

"You left at the end of a workday, had a fine meal, and arrived rested at the destination city at the beginning of the very next workday," he said. "In 1938, that train was, by far, the most efficient use of time for a senior executive who needed to go between the two most important commercial centers in the country. In the late 1940s and 1950s, however, the economic rationale for the passenger train fell apart.

U.S. high-speed rail-corridor designations

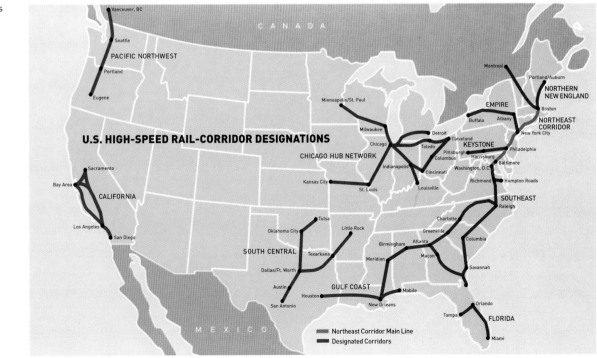

We all know why. The airplane became 'the most efficient use' of a businessperson's time."[11] Withuhn also said: "It is a myth that railroads didn't try to recapture the elusive rail passenger in those days. The railroads did try, and very hard. The railroads didn't abandon us. We, one by one in our individual choices, abandoned them."[12] To succeed in a new century, "trains today must offer the intercity traveler new choices, in a world that is valuing time in a way unprecedented in history."

In the twentieth century there were three distinct eras of political decision-making about passenger rail travel, with the most recent era stretching into the present century.

The previous century began with railroads themselves making most of the decisions. After all, passenger trains were the new technology that was driving travel onward. But for reasons still being debated by academics today, railroads were tightly regulated in the early part of the century. During his presidency (1901–09), Teddy Roosevelt and his trust-busters had done battle with dozens of the old railroad barons, including the legendary Edward Harriman, who was forced to break up his giant combination of the Union Pacific and Southern Pacific Railroads. Out of this era grew the ICC.[13] Then there were the state Public Service Commissions, which also wielded a lot of regulatory power. For instance, during the Great Depression, the California Public Service Commission (PSC) actually ordered the railroads to build a grand new passenger terminal in Los Angeles, partly as a way to create jobs. Thus it is clear that this first era of political decision-making was characterized by a combination of the railroads themselves and the regulatory agencies.

The second era opened in the 1960s as the country became aware that strong-handed

Los Angeles Union Passenger Terminal

government regulation was actually strangling all forms of transportation and creating far more problems than it was solving. "Deregulation" was the watchword of the day. Passenger trains, however, were in a different category. To have fully deregulated them would have effectively eliminated the industry overnight. As we have seen, they were still running only because the ICC and the PSCs would not allow them to be discontinued. Most, but not all, trains had turned into decrepit rust buckets, and many railroads were actively discouraging passengers.[14] Congress decided in 1970 that the only way to save the passenger train was to have the government take over. But that isn't exactly what happened. Instead, congress created Amtrak, which was based on a lie that everyone knew was a lie: Amtrak would operate a scaled-down passenger system efficiently and start turning a profit within two years.

Not only has Amtrak never turned a profit, but it has also absorbed more than $23 billion in federal funds over the past thirty years, and there is no promise of a future profit. During this time, Congress forced Amtrak to run trains into the districts of politically powerful members, voicing support for Amtrak while providing only enough money to keep the trains limping along. Had it not been for dedicated officers and employees who believed in the passenger train, the service would have foundered. Therefore, the second era might be called "the era of political lies and incompetence."

The most fascinating political development, however, has crept in like a fog, overlaying the second era. This third era might be called "the era of smart states and cities." As the federal government sank into partisan bickering, the states began making decisions on transportation policy. Governors and mayors, unlike members of Congress, can't simply wave a magic money wand and order trains to run even if they make no sense in economic terms. At the state and local level, the politicians face real problems, and they must find real solutions. Congestion has become their number-one problem, and it seems ever clearer that the train is one of the solutions.

It is difficult to say which state started the trend. Northeastern states such as New York, New Jersey, and Pennsylvania have always relied on commuter trains, but they have begun to promote explosive growth of commuter service in the past few years. Washington state surprised almost everyone with a cooperative effort to create a new high-speed and commuter network as part of a plan to battle congestion on highways and in ports in the Seattle area. Remarkably, state and city governments, the ports of Tacoma and Seattle, the Burlington Northern Railroad, and the business community came together to make the plan work before a crisis developed.

There have been other surprises, such as North Carolina and Virginia, where serious projects to improve the railroads were under way at the beginning of the century. Virginia not only devoted

Acela Express, interiors, computer-generated images

money to high-speed passenger trains but was also actively discussing plans to attract more rail freight and so take trucks off highways. Likewise, the five states of the Interstate 95 Coalition, from Maryland to New Jersey, had begun a study of whether state funding of railroad improvements could take reduce reliance on trucks and get even more passengers out of their cars. All over the country, projects are breaking out in unexpected places.

Paul Reistrup, the vice president in charge of passenger matters for the eastern freight railroad CSX Transportation, said that, by the end of 2000, his office was working with twenty-nine separate passenger projects around the east and south.[15] But the real granddaddy of state programs is in California. The state that popularized the freeway is spending billions of dollars on rail programs that are quietly revolutionizing passenger travel and freight movement. "California has shown the country the way before, and California may be showing the country the way again," said Bill Schafer, a historian and now a Norfolk Southern Railroad official dealing with state and local governments on passenger and commuter rail.[16]

In some ways, the California rail movement seemed to spring out of the ground. Los Angeles, for example, created a 650-km commuter rail system almost overnight, buying some surplus freight tracks and spending millions to improve freight tracks to also handle commuter trains. While the press concentrated on the problems of Red Line subway construction, the commuter authority Metrolink was suddenly bringing thousands of commuters into Los Angeles from outlying communities. Metrolink continues to grow.

Working through Amtrak, California began subsidizing new passenger trains all over the state, and the Los Angeles–San Diego line is now second to the Northeast Corridor in ridership. Traffic is also growing on lines from San Jose to Sacramento and from Oakland to Bakersfield. Freight railroads have enthusiastically embraced California's plan because the state has pledged enough money not only to prevent passenger trains from interfering with freight service but also to accommodate projected freight growth.

California also is spearheading what is by far the country's largest government-funded freight rail project, the Alameda Corridor, to allow more freight trains to move efficiently to and from the ports of Los Angeles and Long Beach. Thousands of trucks now clog freeways in the area, moving marine containers to local rail yards for transfer to trains.

As the new century began, California released its Rail System Five-Year Improvement Plan, which commits to $4 billion in rail improvements in the period 2000–05. The plan quoted Governor Gray Davis: "Rail is a vital component of California's transportation system. Increasingly, it represents the most efficient and practical means of reducing congestion in our urban transportation corridors."[17]

Paul Reistrup sees the mass of serious passenger rail projects as an indication that the country has seen the value of a mode of transportation that uses very little land compared with highways and airports, and that already has lines into the center of most towns and cities. "The railroad right-of-ways are so valuable that I don't see them going away," he said. "And the stations are in the right places."

The politics of congestion is only one of the factors helping the passenger train to survive in the twenty-first century. Economics is another major factor. Adding a new track to a railroad system, or even building a new rail line, could generally be done for $1,000,000 to $2,000,000 (1.6 km) at the beginning of the new century. Adding a new lane to a freeway cost roughly ten times more, depending on topography and other factors. Building a new freeway in urban areas is almost impossibly expensive even when it can be done.

Then there is the matter of the environment and energy. Passenger trains already have many environmental friends, including such groups as the Sierra Club, who see them as an alternative to the automobile, with the track using far less space per kilometer than the highway. But environmental and energy concerns will become even more important as the century progresses. The world's supply of oil will not last for ever.

The Federal Transportation Advisory Group, in a report to President George W. Bush early in 2001, predicted that overall transportation demand will double in the next twenty years and triple in the next fifty. The group is made up of some of the brightest minds in research and transportation from such groups as the Transportation Research Board, NASA, the Transportation Department, and the National Science and Technology Council.[18]

One of the surprises in the charts and graphs accompanying the group's report was the assumption that high-speed passenger trains will be a part of the future solution. In fact, the charts place airline travel and high-speed rail in the same category, making no distinction between them. The report said that a "new vision" will be necessary and that one of the key requirements of this is "a transportation system that is not dependent on foreign energy and is compatible with the environment." The U.S. transportation system consumes 12,500,000 barrels of oil a day, contributing to greenhouse gases and dependence on foreign oil. Again, one of the solutions outlined by the group is electrically powered trains or new energy sources that would fit trains quite well, such as fuel-cell technology or hydrogen fuel.

"We're going to have a humongous energy crisis in the twenty-first century unless we can come up with alternative forms of energy," Bill Schafer said, although he is "not 100% convinced that it's going to be electricity that run trains." Electric power doubles the cost of building or improving railroads, and

Metro subway system,
Washington, D.C., 1966

politicians and industry are just now beginning to understand that global warming is real, he explained. Fuel cells, fusion, or even advanced batteries, he believes, may play a role in railroading's future.

Like the historians and transportation specialists interviewed for this essay, the Federal Transportation Advisory Group stressed that the country can no longer think in terms of separate forms of transportation: trains, planes, ships, and automobiles. All forms of transportation must be integrated into an "intermodal" system in which people and freight can easily use a combination of modes "economically [to] move anyone and anything anywhere, anytime, on time," the report said.

Already, this is beginning to happen. Freight railroads, ports, and trucking companies were leading the way at the beginning of the new century. Oddly, passenger companies were only grudgingly coming around. For instance, the Air Transport Association continued to fight against the use of any airline or airport taxes for airport access, seeing rail links and even highway links as someone else's problem—and someone else's budget. Most people seemed to consider intermodalism to be parking lots at transit stations.

But, here and there, real intermodalism was breaking out in the passenger world. New York continued to debate rail access to La Guardia and Kennedy airports, as did some other airports. Washington's Reagan National Airport built a new terminal that reached out to incorporate the Metro rail-transit station. At Newark, New Jersey, Continental Airlines and Amtrak appeared to be creeping toward the first true combination of services. Aware that the summer of 2000 would be a time of terrible delays, Continental made a deal with Amtrak to take delayed passengers to destinations along the Washington–New York–Boston Northeast Corridor. It was so pleased with the results that it extended the contract. The Northeast Corridor runs less than 0.5 kilometers from the Newark air terminals, and a new monorail is being built to connect the terminals to a new passenger station on the Corridor. There is nothing new, however, about train–plane intermodalism, and U.S. airlines have a number of through-ticketing agreements with European rail systems. Many European airports have train stations beneath them. But these same American airlines entered the new century with no such agreements in the U.S.A.

What will the passenger train of 2099 look like? The consensus seems to be that it will look pretty much like it looks today, although more aerodynamic and filled with new equipment, new alloys, and new safety systems that will allow much faster speeds. And there is general agreement that it will ride on steel wheels on steel rails, although both will be much improved.

Despite the federal government's support of magnetic levitation as the twentieth century ended, there is an overwhelming chorus of negativism when the subject is mentioned around historians, experienced railroaders, or long-time observers. "I see no future for maglev or anything like it," said Mark Hemphill, editor of Trains magazine. "The drawbacks to this technology are inherent and thus insoluble, and no amount of research or money spent will do anything more than minimize their effects. These include coping with debris on the track, difficulty of operation in inclement weather, a much more onerous requirement for perfect alignment everywhere all the time, a fabulously expensive infrastructure that cannot be installed incrementally, and most of all, a failure to demonstrate a real service or cost advantage over existing wheel-on-rail technology. Maglev is another dream like the supersonic transport: if it was such a good idea, it would have happened already. But since it can't demonstrate an obvious cost or service advantage, it will likely remain experimental only and eventually be dropped as unworkable."[19]

A number of experts pointed to the New York subway system, which has been in the ground for more than a century but still is running on steel rails. "It is cleaner and quieter, but it's running pretty much the same," John Hankey said. He and others noted that the country has better things on which to spend its money than a new type of subway or a new type of railroad. "There's no better technology in the ground than what's there now," is Bill Schafer's view.

None of this is to say that railroad technology will not improve. The locomotives, cars, rail, signal systems, and other hardware and communications equipment in use at the beginning of the the new century were vastly better than those of the beginning of the twentieth. And in just the past three decades, there has been as much improvement as during the previous seven. The improvement has not looked as dramatic as the switch from steam locomotives to diesels, but nevertheless it has been dramatic. Diesel-locomotive technology has leapt forward with such changes as the development of more powerful and more reliable alternating-current locomotive drive systems. Many new diesels still look the same and sound the same, but they are not. An increasing number have diagnostic systems that can detect defects and send a message to the repair shop before the engineer realizes anything is wrong. Electric locomotives used on Amtrak's Northeast Corridor and in other parts of the world have such amenities as cruise control. Rail now comes out of the rolling mills with better wear characteristics but also free of the microscopic air bubbles that once grew into cracks that caused derailments.

Exciting new concepts are coming, sooner rather than later, such as "positive train control," which would take control of the train away from the engineer if he or she made a mistake or exceeded the speed limit.[20] Plastic or composite crossties may replace wood or concrete. New alloys, new wheel shapes, and new wheel–rail dynamics have allowed ever higher speeds. Engineers are now persuaded there is no real limit to the speed of wheeled trains, and by the end of the century they may be going nearly as fast as current airliners.

The crystal ball grows murky, however, if one asks a different question about the future of rail travel. Will there still be a "national" passenger train system with not only high-speed, short-distance trains but also long-distance trains hauling sleeping cars, diners, and lounge cars? Again a consensus emerged from the people interviewed for this article: unless Congress continues to force them to run, long-distance passenger trains will fade away as basic transportation and become cruise trains to show travelers the country's scenic wonders. But the shorter-distance, high-speed train will take on a greater role than most people imagine. "I think passenger trains will slowly but steadily increase their role, and within fifty years become the dominant form of public transportation in the one-to-three-hour market—that is, the 160–800-km corridor," Mark Hemphill said. "The technology can absorb enormous increases in passenger load and frequency of service, whereas the U.S. is rapidly approaching saturation in aircraft transportation. I don't see the public accepting too many more multi-billion-dollar airports due to environmental and quality-of-life considerations, and without new airports the system will very quickly reach saturation. Similarly, Interstate highways cannot be doubled or tripled in size, or paralleled, without encountering what are likely to be impossible political challenges."

"In the plus-800-km market," he added, "I expect aircraft to remain dominant due to time considerations. We're not going to see the resurgence of long-haul or overnight passenger trains on the 1950s model. They're too time-consuming for most travelers and simply too expensive. The streamliner of the 1950s had a market purely because there wasn't an acceptable alternative, and when that alternative arose, their market evaporated. The overnight-train market will continue to be a 'the trip is the destination' market for tours and as a scenic or luxury experience, but will never become day-to-day transportation for business and regular travelers."

Others generally agreed. "I can't see it [long-distance trains] beyond the cruise train status," Bill Schafer said. But not everyone was totally pessimistic. Reistrup could envision long-distance trains, although they would "change in character" to "a cross between higher-speed and tilt trains." Despite all the predictions, there is no guarantee that everyone who is certain will also be correct. Hankey calls the U.S.A. "a vast experiment in unintended consequences."

1 Interviews with Hankey, December 1999 and January 2000.
2 William L. Withuhn, *Rails Across America: A History of Railroads in North America*, New York (Smithmark Publishers Inc.) 1993.
3 William D. Middleton, *When the Steam Railroads Electrified*, Milwaukee (Kalmbach Publishing Co.) 1974.
4 S. Kip Farrington Jr., *Railroads at War*, New York (Coward-McCann Inc.) 1944, and Ron Ziel, *Steel Rails to Victory*, New York (Hawthorn Books) 1970.
5 Mike Schafer and Joe Welsh, *Classic American Streamliners*, Osceola WI (MBI Publishing Co.) 1997.
6 Fred W. Frailey, *Twilight of the Great Trains*, Milwaukee (Kalmbach Publishing Co.) 1998.
7 Gordon Gill, *Amtrak: Long-distance Service, Can it be Made Viable?*, Pittsburgh (Dorn Publishing) 1998, and Interstate Commerce Commission, Docket 31954, Report 306ICC417, 1959.
8 Claiborne Pell, *Megalopolis Unbound: The Supercity and the Transportation of Tomorrow*, New York (Frederick A. Praeger) 1966.
9 Harold A. Edmonson, *Journey to Amtrak: The Year that History Rode the Passenger Train*, Milwaukee (Kalmbach Publishing Co.) 1972.
10 American Public Transportation Association, annual transit report, April 16, 2001.
11 Interviews with Withuhn, December 1999 and January 2000.
12 Withuhn, speech to National Corridors Initiative, Washington, D.C., June 2000.
13 Donovan L. Hofsommer, *The Southern Pacific: 1901–1985*, College Station TX (Texas A & M University Press) 1986.
14 Harold A. Edmonson, *Journey to Amtrak, The Year that History Rode the Passenger Train*, Milwaukee (Kalmbach Publishing Co.) 1972.
15 Interviews with Reistrup, January and February 2000.
16 Interviews with Schafer, January and February 2000.
17 Coast Rail Coordinating Council, *California Passenger Rail System Five-Year Improvement Plan Summary Report*, Draft Final, May 15, 2000, revised June 15, 2000.
18 Federal Transportation Advisory Group, *Vision 2050: An Integrated Transportation System*, February. 5, 2001.
19 Written comments from Hemphill in response to author's questions, January 9, 2000.
20 U.S. Department of Transportation, *The Changing Face of Transportation*, BTS00-07, Washington, D.C.

THE PROJECTS

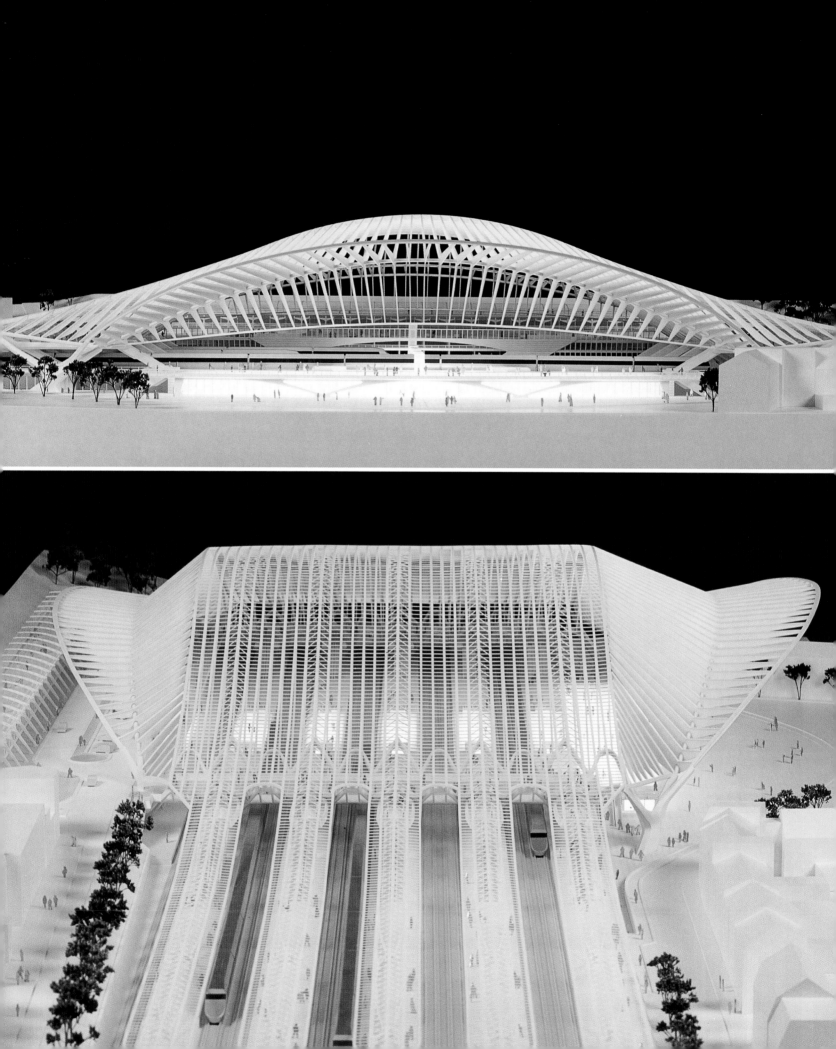

LIÈGE-GUILLEMINS STATION, LIÈGE, BELGIUM

Architect: Santiago Calatrava

Engineer: Santiago Calatrava

Expected completion: 2006

1 Model, view toward entrance

2 Model, view from above toward platforms

3 Transversal section

4 Longitudinal section

Liège is situated in the eastern part of Belgium, and plans for Liège-Guillemins Station were developed after the extension of railway high-speed lines linking London, Paris, Brussels, Amsterdam, and points in Germany. The old station of Liège could not satisfy the new requirements for high-speed travel and the increasing number of passengers. An entirely new station therefore had to be built that included a remodeling of the track system in the area. As an added criterion of the design, the new building needed to connect two very different parts of the city: Colline de Cointe, a quiet residential hillside area, and Guillemins, a busy district including retail services.

Santiago Calatrava was the winner of a Europe-wide competition for the design of the new station. He proposed a mainly transparent building, consisting of a steel and glass vault, using a system of monumental ribs that accentuate the structure. In some ways it is reminiscent of classical stations, but turned sideways. Main entrances are on two sides: one facing the new pedestrian square at the front, and the other facing the mountainside at the rear, where the parking is located. Large canopies creating a porch-like effect crown the entrances.

The site of the new station, approximately 200 meters away from the existing station, has a significant slope. Parts of the building are underground at the rear while being visible at the front side. The entrance at the front of the station leads to the concourse, which contains the travel center, information and welcome desk, left-luggage facilities, and retail areas. An adjacent subway will connect the concourse to the five platforms, serving all kinds of railway traffic on nine tracks. The first platform will widen into a terrace above the main entrance; the other four are 8 meters wide and three of these are 450 meters long, to accommodate the double-deck French high-speed TGV trains.

Another access to the platforms is provided by two footbridges, which span the tracks at the rear side of the station and end at the ground level. In the underground part of the building, there is parking space for approximately 800 cars, with the lowest level also linked with the subway under the tracks. Above the parking garage, a two-floor steel-and-glass construction clings to the slope, leaving space for a drop-off zone next to the rear station entrance.

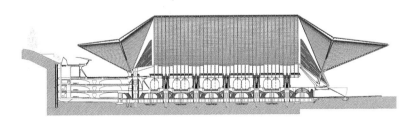

3

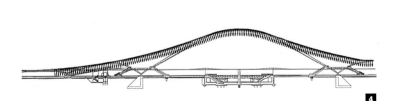

4

A special feature, unique in Europe, is a bridge that gives direct vehicular access from the nearby motorway to this zone, allowing automobile travelers to avoid the crowded area in front of the station. The first floor of the building projecting toward the hill will be occupied by travelers' services such as car-rental companies. Visitors will be able to enjoy the panoramic view over the mountainside from the second floor. Rooms for staff and management will be located beneath the drop-off area, with windows allowing views into the station. Departments managing the travel center and other technical concerns are located under platform one. Separate gangways for employees will facilitate easy movement between the working quarters. Together the subway, footbridges, and various elevators, escalators, staircases, and gangways are parts of a well-thought-out system of communication throughout the station.

The track system around the station will be reorganized to allow trains to enter at 100 kph instead of the former 40 kph. The definitive location of the new building was chosen to unite Place des Guillemins, in front of the old station, and the future station square. The similar-looking canopies at the rear and front of the new station will stress the equally important role of both sides. As the predominantly transparent design prevents the structure acting as a wedge, the whole building seeks to be a visual and effective link crossing over the tracks. Calatrava's design is like a bridge, meeting the demand for a connection between the two different parts of Liège.

5 Preliminary sketch for structural system

6 Preliminary sketch for vault

7 Model, overall view

8 Model, entrance area

9 Model, partial view of canopy and platform area

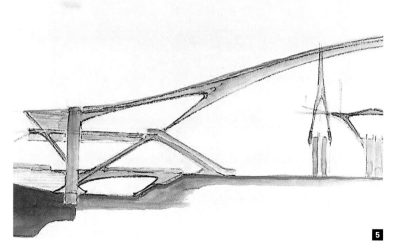

5

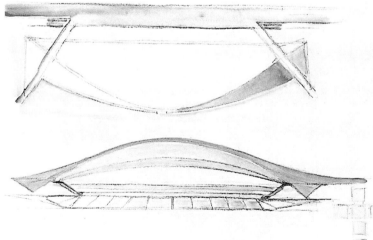

6

HUNG HOM STATION, KOWLOON, HONG KONG, CHINA

Architects: Foster and Partners

Consultants: Arup, WT Partnership
Construction completed: 1998

The firm of British architect Sir Norman Foster was commissioned by the Kowloon Canton Railway Corporation to renovate extensively and enlarge the existing station to meet increased demand and to cope with the introduction of new double-deck trains running between mainland China and Hong Kong. The old station was built in the mid-1970s and experienced a series of *ad hoc* additions and modifications over time in a futile effort to meet the increasing demand of more than 150,000 passengers a day. The new station addition, which doubles existing space, is divided into three levels: track at the ground level, public walkways at mid-level, and a concourse on a raised podium. It will service more than 500 train arrivals and departures a day and will provide a transport interchange for buses, taxis, and private cars.

A main goal was to enlarge the concourse area, but to encourage its

1   Night view of glazed pavilion extension

2   Interior view of station concourse

3   Interior detail of roof

2▶

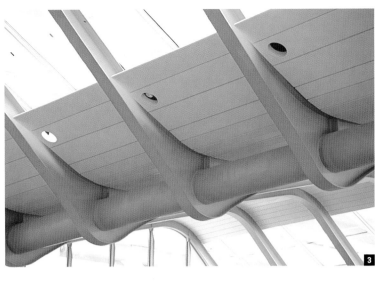

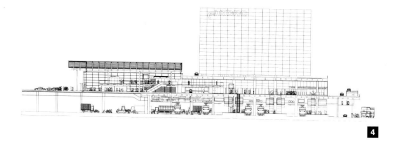

4

5

use by mainly international passengers, who need to pass through customs and immigration services. Distinct zones were therefore created for international departures, international arrivals, and domestic travelers. Daily commuters enter and exit via the mid-level walkways, increasing ease and efficiency of movement. The station has been expanded eastward with a new lightweight pavilion, doubling the size of the concourse. The new building is covered by a dramatic wave-form roof made of steel that has transparent panels supported by a light steel structure. The linear roof lights and full-height glazed curtain wall further draw attention to the roof. Platforms, public walkways, and concourses are connected by atrium voids that penetrate through all levels of the building, allowing natural light to reach the platforms below. The new project brought higher, international standards to the elements of signage, ticketing facilities, escalators, and lighting. As in many Foster designs, a simple, elegant gesture creates a startling, new, and efficient landmark.

4 East-west section

5 East elevation

6, 7, 8 Interior views of station concourse

6

7

8 ▶

KOWLOON STATION, HONG KONG, CHINA

Architect: Terry Farrell and Partners

Engineers: Arup

Construction completed: 1997

The Mass Transit Railway Corporation (MTRC) has created a completely new connection between the center of Hong Kong and the new airport at Chek Lap Kok. The new rail link is a 34-km route with a large part constructed on reclaimed land. Kowloon Station is the largest station on the route and is part of the master plan by the British firm of Terry Farrell and Partners to create a transportation super city in West Kowloon. The development area of 13.5 hectares will, when completed, contain over 1,000,000 square meters of hotel, office, retail, and residential accommodation, organized around a main square that has Kowloon Station at its core. The station is intended not only to serve the transport needs of the area, but is also conceived as the central focus of the area, contributing to its identity.

Kowloon Station is a transit interchange bringing together three rail lines, airport check-in facilities, and bus and other road transportation. Each element is linked by a central concourse, which, in turn, is connected by an atrium to the development above and around the station. From a distance, the station reveals a sweeping, curved roof that creates a distinctive reference point, in spite of the fact that it will be the lowest building in the development area. The roof is "anchored" by four towers that create a monumental open space between them, a gateway to the stations. Under ground, the form and geometry are highly rational and straightforward. The station functions fit within a structure of 300 meters by 180 meters known as "the box," subdivided by modules of 12 square meters each. It is constructed of reinforced concrete and incorporates three suspended levels above ground and two levels below ground. The functions are organized

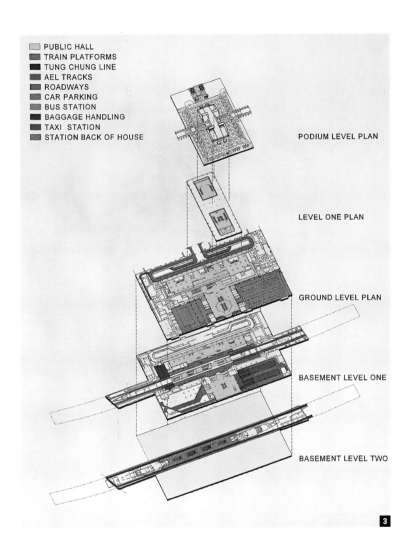

PUBLIC HALL
TRAIN PLATFORMS
TUNG CHUNG LINE
AEL TRACKS
ROADWAYS
CAR PARKING
BUS STATION
BAGGAGE HANDLING
TAXI STATION
STATION BACK OF HOUSE

PODIUM LEVEL PLAN

LEVEL ONE PLAN

GROUND LEVEL PLAN

BASEMENT LEVEL ONE

BASEMENT LEVEL TWO

3

1   Main station entrance

2   In-town check-in hall

3   Dissected axonometric indicating levels
    and uses

1
2

by floor: train platforms at the lowest levels; arrivals level with internal drop-off roads and in-town check-in for airport passengers; departure level associated with taxis, buses, and private car park; station entry from the surrounding developments; and the uppermost level, which allows entry directly from the area called Kowloon Station Square.

At Kowloon Station, a central concourse resolved the problem of providing complex interconnections between the rail lines and other modes of transport. The station uses an abundance of escalators, concentrated in the central open areas for a visually dynamic effect, but, more importantly, to concentrate vertical movement in a single volume, thereby contributing to the easy understanding of the organization of the space. The architects have used extensive glass to make this space a great, light-filled hall that allows natural light to penetrate to the levels below. This single large space, filled with movement and meeting and greeting of passengers, is an echo of grand stations of a bygone era. However, the traditional vocabulary of train stations stops there. The train itself is not seen from the station areas. Rather, an emphasis is placed on the traveler and the services needed: more like a modern airport.

4

4 Section and urban context

5 Overall view at night

6 Concourse

COTE ARRIVEE

AXE VOIES T.G.V

VERS PARIS

VERS MARSEILLE

COTE DEPART

RD 9

AIX EN PROVENCE

VERS VITROLLES

RD 9

ET MARIGNANE

ARBOIS TGV STATION, AIX-EN-PROVENCE, FRANCE

Architects: SNCF/Jean-Marie Duthilleul, Etienne Tricaud, and Pierre Saboya

Engineers: AREP, ARCORA, EEG-Trouvin

Expected completion: 2001

The Arbois TGV Station is located in a large population catchment area that includes Aix-en-Provence and its surrounding region, as well as the communities of Marignane, Vitrolles, and Rognac. It is projected that twenty trains will stop at this regional station daily. The train station is positioned at the intersection of the TGV rail line and the road linking Aix-en-Provence with Marignane. This road passes below the rail line and splits into two one-way lanes. Access ramps allow motorists to connect to a service road that circles the TGV facilities.

The station itself is a low structure with a sweeping, wave-shaped roof that rises up in the center and slopes down at both ends. The building contains travel services, the central platform area, and walkways allowing pedestrians to cross the tracks safely. A lightweight construction was used for the building, which is enclosed by glass walls on two sides. The southern exposure is equipped with "sunbreakers"—wood veneer on glass—to protect against excessive heat from the sun.

The simple, elegant structure is further integrated into the surrounding environment through the landscape plan. Rows of plane trees line the platforms. Other spaces are designed as a Southern French garden dominated by pink laurel bushes. The car park is an important component of this facility as it will cater to many "park-and-ride" travelers. At present it has 700 spaces, but could be extended to provide 1100, and is planted with oaks, in keeping with the surrounding rocky hillside.

1   Overall perspective

2   Site plan

3   Longitudinal section

4   Transversal section

5   View of interior overlooking platforms

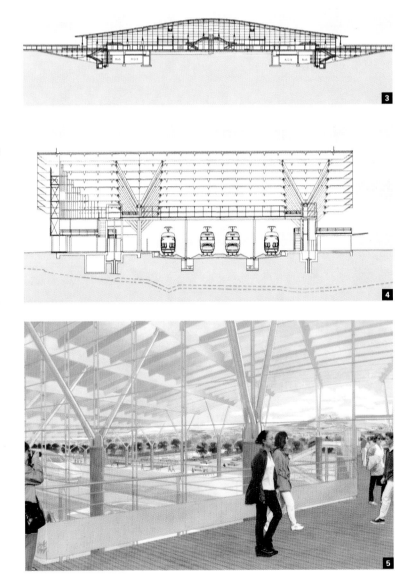

LILLE–EUROPE TGV STATION, LILLE, FRANCE

Architects: SNCF/Jean-Marie Duthilleul, Etienne Tricaud and Pierre Saboya

Engineers: Peter Rice with Jean-François Blassel of RFR and Sophie Lebourva of Arup
Construction completed: 1994

This intermodal station welcomes the high-speed Eurostar train on its way from London through the Channel Tunnel to Paris or Brussels. It was conceived as part of the larger project of Eurolille, a new city business district intended to create a modern metropolis from the historic city of Lille. The solution, which turned out to be one of the most challenging urban projects of the early 1990s in Europe, was initiated with the plans for the new railway station. The initiative started in 1988 after the projects for the Channel Tunnel and

the new high-speed train route had been sealed. It is a product of a political decision to build up regional cities and support decentralization in France as well as the construction of new regions within the European Union. The venture also seeks to combine public interests with those of private investors in order to encourage economic growth. It is hoped that this growth will be friendly to the local population as well as open to multinational companies looking for a new locations offering modern and accessible space.

The overall concept for Eurolille was designed by the Dutch architect Rem Koolhaas, who was chosen from four French and four international architects. The project combines a series of individual yet interdependent projects for business, retail, and cultural facilities, along with a new transportation center. The following buildings, flanking the railway tracks and the new station by Jean-Marie Duthilleul, have been built: the Crédit Lyonnais Tower by Christian de Portzamparc, the World Trade Center by Claude Vasconi, the Triangle

Commercial Center by Jean Nouvel, and the Lille Grand Palais, a convention and exhibition hall, by Rem Koolhaas.

The railway station, which is the most important component of the newly created town center, is really a transport center that seeks to integrate the new high-speed TGV service with existing modes of transportation, such as bus, subway, and car. The station at first reminds the visitor of a traditional train shed: a transparent and light construction with a curved roof, metal supports,

1   Partial view of platforms

2   View from inside toward the town

3   Lower level platforms

4   Concourse area showing roof structure

5   Preliminary sketch

6   Floor and circulation plans

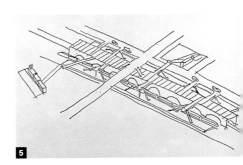

5

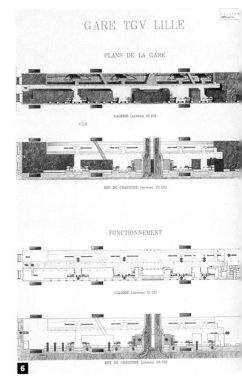

GARE TGV LILLE

PLANS DE LA GARE

GALERIE (niveau 21.15)

REZ DE CHAUSSEE (niveau 25.50)

FONCTIONNEMENT

GALERIE (niveau 21.15)

REZ DE CHAUSSEE (niveau 25.50)

6

and glass walls. The roof has been likened to a flying carpet hovering over the site. The roof skin consists of alternating transverse bands of glazing and metal cladding. Beneath the skin is hung a flexible sheet of perforated aluminum that allows daylight to filter through. A feeling of lightness has been achieved through a structure of slender tubular arches. These help create an interior space that is reminiscent of traditional train stations.

Built on a sloping site, the station has three levels. Visitors enter at street level and immediately view the great concourse below. One level below the concourse, trains arrive and depart. This space is articulated with steel trusses, struts, and bracing, as well as the many elements of station furniture, such as kiosks, benches, and escalators. Adjacent parking facilities are also below ground. Transparency and openness of spaces are concepts expressed throughout the railway station. Everything strives to promote access to different modes of transportation and easy communication between these and the city. The transparent walls enable passengers to be embraced by the city while connecting them with the activity in the surrounding town even before they exit the station. The Place de l'Europe, a great urban space in front of the transport station at the lower level, with a shopping mall alongside, promises to be a vibrant public gathering place for viewing the trains as well as the silhouette of the old town.

3 **4**

EOLE HAUSSMAN-ST-LAZARE STATION, PARIS, FRANCE

Architects: SNCF/Jean-Marie Duthilleul, Etienne Tricaud, and Roland Legrand

Engineers: AREP, Setec, TPI, Simecsol and Sogelerg

Construction completed: 1999

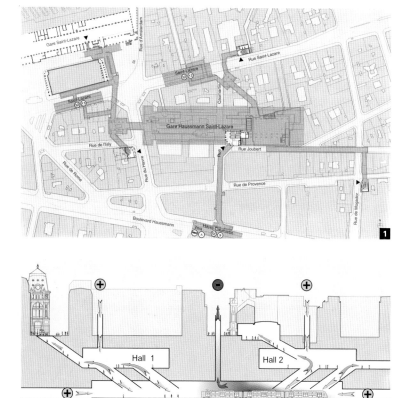

The regional express line EOLE has led to the building of two major urban-transportation facilities in the north of Paris. The first 2.8-km portion of this system opened in July 1999 and provides a rapid link between Gare du Nord and Gare St-Lazare. The completely underground EOLE stations, Haussmann-St-Lazare and Magenta, represent a bold approach to the future of stations in the modern city. These new stations will serve as rail interchanges for the suburban train service and the Métro, and will connect to long-distance train stations.

The new underground station Haussman-St-Lazare is an enormous complex located in the 8th and 9th *arrondissements* of Paris, in the heart of a vital business district near office, department stores, the Opéra and Gare St-Lazare. The new facility will serve riders on four Métro lines, the regional express line, the future Meteor Métro line, and travelers connecting to the long-distance trains at nearby Gare St-Lazare. The exchange hubs of the new station are located in two large halls: the Caumartin hall and Le Havre hall. The Caumartin hall is a space of 3000 square meters with a megastructure that takes the form of immense bracing beams and joist. The entrances and exits to the two EOLE stations are not typical subway entrances located on pedestrian sidewalks. Rather, the city authorities required that access be through entrance halls in the ground level of certain buildings.

In contrast to surface-level stations, where the passenger can directly relate to the surrounding town or city, in an underground station the spaces are often poor and orientation is difficult. It is as if time

1 Site plan

2 Section showing underground halls

3,4 View of the underground halls

3 ▶
4 ▶

5   View of the underground halls

6   Platforms

7   Hall

spent under ground is considered unimportant. In the case of the new EOLE underground stations, it is believed that these spaces should create a rich and memorable environment, especially as people spend more and more time traveling beneath the city. For the stations, the architects based their design on the following fundamental components: form and scale, structure, light, materials, and color. The construction is not considered as a single building, but rather a sequence of spaces.

The construction of a completely underground station was an engineering feat, because of the magnitude of the underground spaces and tunnels that had to be excavated. The large halls were built as open-cut works. The wall supports were installed; further down, barrel vaults were used for the large spaces and catenary vaults for narrower passages. In projects such as EOLE, the civil-engineering part uses up about 90% of the budget. The architects therefore sought to make the spaces defined by the structures as expressive as possible and chose materials carefully and located them where they would create a useful and hospitable environment. The station is characterized by its construction of concrete poured *in situ*, with various types of finishes. Wood and metal are used for walkways. Wood is also used for treads on escalators and the generous benches on the platforms. Copper is used on the façades of mechanical rooms. The overall lighting scheme creates a counterpoint to the power of the visible structural elements and further reduces the impression of enclosure. Giant hanging colored lamps send up light that reflects off the vaults, and this is complemented by lighting on walls and columns.

LEHRTER STATION, BERLIN, GERMANY

Architect: Meinhard von Gerkan of von Gerkan, Marg + Partners

Engineers: Schlaich, Bergermann and Partners; IVZ/Emsch + Berger

Expected completion: 2006

1 Computer rendering, view through glass roof toward platforms

2 Longitudinal section

3 Model, view toward elevated tracks and two buildings with concourse in between

Planned for up to 30,000,000 passengers a year and thus to become the largest station in the city, Lehrter Station is meant to create a major transportation center for the country, contribute the revitalization of a part of Berlin, and serve the nearby new governmental district with its thousands of daily commuters. It is being constructed on the site of the former nineteenth-century station. During the Nazi regime this was destined to become the grandiose termination of the northern point of the north–south axis of the capital city and as such became a target of allied bombings. Two high-speed ICE rail tracks will cross at this point, one north–south, the other east–west, forming connections within Germany that will eventually become part of the two most important European routes: from Scandinavia to Sicily and from Moscow to London. The station will also be a stop on the new north–south underground (U-Bahn) track and the east–west suburban line (S-Bahn).

The plans for a new monumental station were developed after the reunification of Germany and the decision to make Berlin once again the capital city. Ideas for the station were solicited in 1993 from two German architects, Meinhard von Gerkan and Professor J.P. Kleihues. Von Gerkan's scheme was selected to be developed. Many challenges faced the architects. It was explicitly stated that the new station should not be a shopping center with rail links. Although it occupies an enormous site, it should be transparent, open, and inviting to pedestrians. The engineering difficulties of realigning tracks, constructing on the banks of the Spree River, and accommodating three different types of rail service in one station added to the challenge.

The station complex is an important and visible component of the area's redevelopment plans. It is set apart from the other buildings, thus taking on a symbolic role in the composition of the new area. The organization of the station complex is surprisingly straightforward and reflects the crossing railways. There

2 ▶
3 ▶

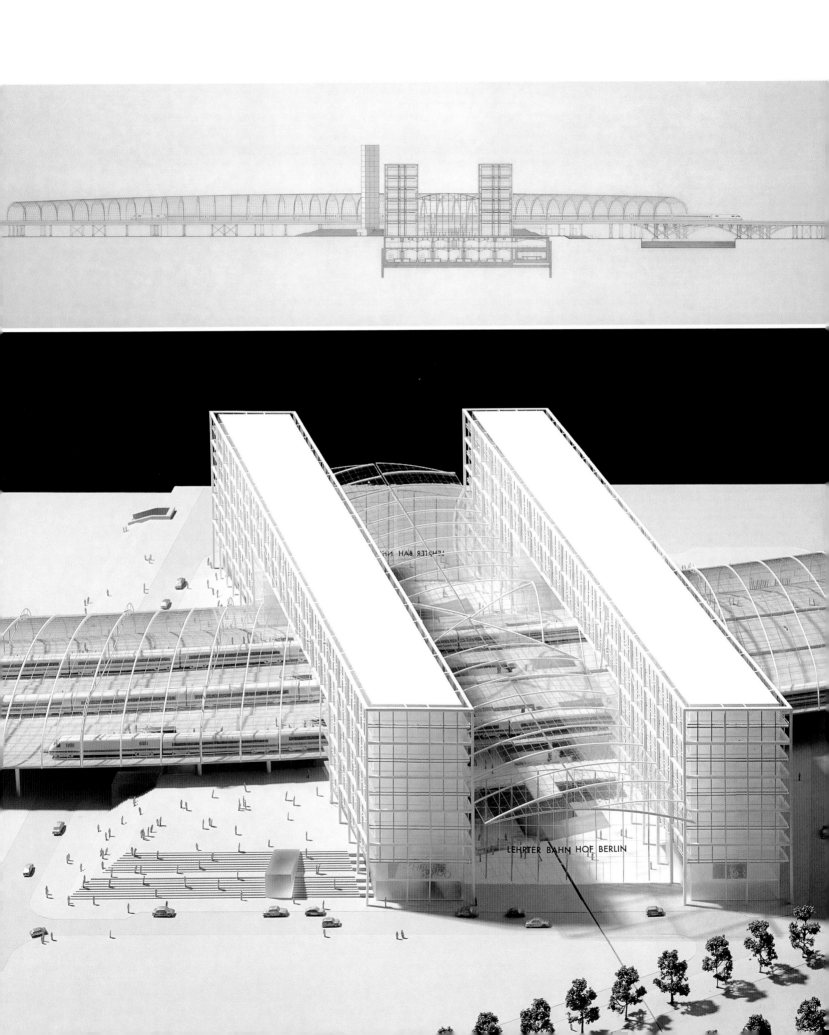

are tracks for the S-Bahn city train and the high-speed trains in the east–west direction 10 meters above the street level; taxi, bus, car, and pedestrian accesses at the street level and 15 meters below the subway; and high-speed train tracks in the north–south direction. A barrel-vaulted glass roof 430 meters long covers the elevated east–west tracks. This construction covering the platforms cuts across two rectangular buildings that contain retail and service facilities and a hotel. Between these "slab" buildings is the main station's multilevel concourse. The central hall of 170 meters by 50 meters makes extensive use of glass-and-steel construction to allow as much daylight as possible to penetrate to the lowest floors. Its design seeks to convey a feeling of lightness and transparency, expressed through the modular tensile cable structure, and at the same time to retain the skeleton structure of traditional train sheds. The whole complex is unified by the creation of a rectangular plinth, almost 4.5 meters above street level, that frames the complex and forms public open space for pedestrians.

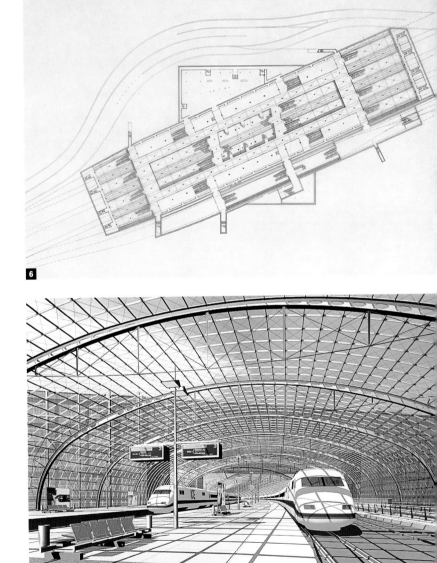

6

4 Model, east-west elevated tracks and twin buildings

5 View into main hall

6 Plan of ground floor

7 View under glass roof of platforms

COLOGNE–BONN AIRPORT RAILWAY STATION, GERMANY

Architect: Helmut Jahn, Murphy/Jahn

Engineer: Werner Sobek

Expected completion: 2003

1   Model, airport with station

2   Model, view at night of station roof

3   Perspective at platform level

The project for a new railway station at Cologne-Bonn Airport is a part of a competition that took place in 1992 for the enlargement and modernization of the passenger facilities of the existing airport. German-born and Chicago-located Helmut Jahn won the overall master-plan competition and is the architect of Terminal 2 and the new railway station. A parallel goal linked to the airport's modernization was to contribute to bringing new economic activity to the region after the transfer of the capital from Bonn to Berlin. In the past, Cologne-Bonn focused on cargo transport and it is now the second-largest freight airport in Germany. It is also looking to expand its role in passenger transportation. The rail connection is critical to future efficiency and expansion. Located close to the much larger airport of Düsseldorf and within one hour's travel via high-speed train of Frankfurt Airport, Cologne-Bonn has much future potential.

Airport expansion plans include a third terminal (Terminal 2 opened in 2000) and two large multilevel parking garages for 5800 and 4300 cars, as well as the new railway station. It is hoped that local and long-distance passengers will increasingly travel by train, thus avoiding parking problems. Further considerations in favor of the new rail connection are convenience for passengers, the transport of airport personnel, higher reliability, and ecological concerns.

In order to protect the environment as much as possible a decision was made to build one-third of the whole line within a tunnel below the ground. The railway station is situated between Terminal 2 and the planned Terminal 3, parallel to the old Terminal 1. It is meant to serve high-speed trains as well as subway and local lines. Two high-speed trains and three local trains in each direction are planned to serve the station. The old roads serving Terminal 1, running in the middle of the two new terminals, were torn down and realigned at the perimeter of the new buildings in order to free up the space needed for the railway station.

The station is basically two sections of concrete tunnel with a central portion covered with a glass roof. The four tracks are built within a tunnel 18 meters below the ground. The architect decided to open the tunnel and cover it with a shallow shed made of a light steel structure supported by cables. Perhaps inspired by the structure of a bicycle wheel, this support system expresses the reliability of each element of the structure, while emphasizing the delicacy of the minimalist cables. The glass roof extends for approximately 150 meters of the total 400-meter length of the new construction. During the day it allows light to

enter the station area. At night it is like a glowing strip in the airport landscape. The station is completely open inside, and only at the very ends is it divided into levels that lead to Terminal 2, and to Terminal 1 and the planned Terminal 3, respectively. Passengers riding on the trains and coming out of the tunnel encounter a surprisingly light-filled and open station hall. The whole station functions as a linear route to the airport, while the architect's vocabulary reflects his continuing interests in the possibilities of glass and the expression of the building's sophisticated structure.

4   Model, glass roof of station and airport terminal 2

5   Longitudinal section

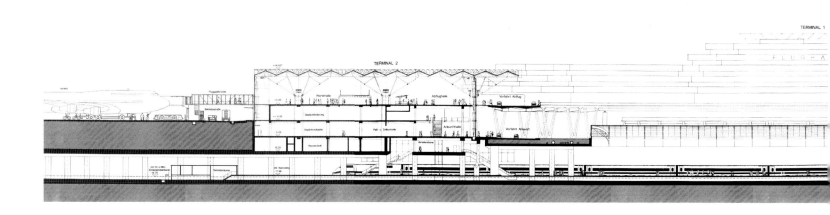

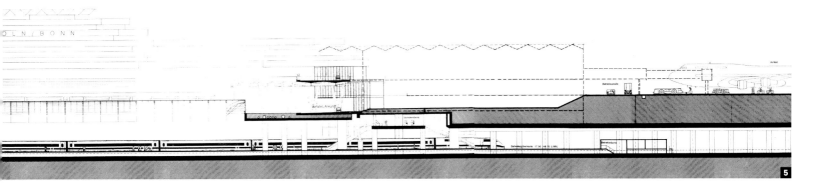

FRANKFURT AIRPORT ICE-RAILWAY STATION
FRANKFURT AM MAIN, GERMANY

Architects: Bothe–Richter–Teherani

Engineers: Ingenieurbüro Binnewies, HL-Technik AG

Construction completed, phase I: 2000

1 View from airport toward station

2 Model, bird's-eye view

3 Model, view at night

4 Site plan

Frankfurt Airport, with 40,000,000 passengers a year, is the eighth largest in the world and one of the most important air-traffic nodes in Europe. Since 1972 it has been connected with the center of the city by local trains and is the first one that has a direct high-speed rail link, which is a result of a joint decision by the German federal railway, Deutsche Bahn, and Frankfurt am Main Airport. In the hope of profiting from a constantly increasing number of passengers (growing by about 5% a year), it was decided to build a new station terminal that would serve high-speed electric trains only, to meet a projected demand of 9,000,000 passengers a year.

The winning entry of the competition was the German architectural firm Bothe–Richter–Teherani. BRT is known for its fluid approach to building forms, and its scheme resembles a "space ship," clad in metal with randomly placed perforations to allow light to enter. Although the building cannot be considered complete, the new station is already a striking construction. It is built as an autonomous structure parallel to the main airport building.

A covered pedestrian bridge connects the two buildings, which are separated by a motorway. The station, 700 meters long, is essentially a concrete-and-steel platform carried by aluminum-clad V-shaped supports. From afar it looks very much like a mechanical millipede. The central portion is covered with a spectacular glass dome, signaling its railway function.

The building currently has three levels. The upper level is the concourse area, welcoming arriving air passengers. The intermediate level houses lounges for Lufthansa

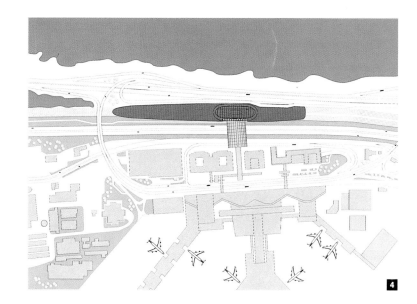

4

3

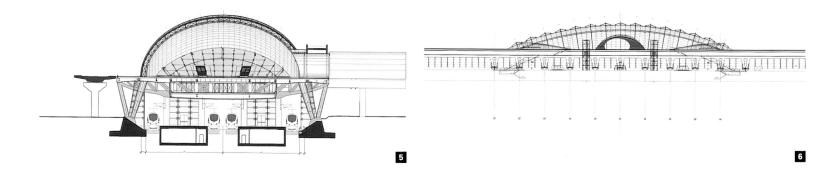

5

6

and railway club passengers, tourist services, and shopping facilities. The lower level, flanked by the supports, is reserved for two platforms with two rail tracks each. A dramatic elliptical opening extending from the upper level down to the platforms allows passengers to view the trains and permits natural light to pass down to that level. The architects, who like to stress the object-like character of the building, designed it so that it can easily be enlarged. The foundations can carry up to twelve more stories. There are plans to enlarge the station under a continuous membrane if

demand for an entertainment center is realized.

The form of the station expresses its function. It looks like a UFO that just landed on the airport. It is not a place that caters just to the simple needs of train travelers, but instead considers passengers of the future. This "unidentified flying object" is supposed to become an "unlimited free-time object" that will accommodate retail outlets, services, and leisure activities. It is planned so that it can expand according to the future needs.

7

5   Transversal section

6   Longitudinal section

7   Rendering of platforms and
    opening above

8   Main level with elliptical opening
    to platforms

9   Stairs and elevator from
    platforms to upper level

8

9

MAIN STATION, STUTTGART, GERMANY

Architects: Ingenhoven, Overdiek, and Partners

Structural engineering specialist adviser: Frei Otto

Estimated construction: 2002-08

1 Cutaway model

2 Model, view of platform area

3, 4 Light studies for dispersal of daylight

The idea for a complete reconstruction of the existing main station of the German city of Stuttgart is one of a series of planned overall adaptations of the railway system to high-speed travel in Germany. New rail tracks will be built and the existing terminus will be converted into a through station in order to enable departing trains to attain higher velocities immediately after leaving the station. The tracks, which will run 12 meters below the street level, will also save precious city land for development, parks, and access roads. The existing rail tracks will be abandoned and become free for redevelopment.

Deutsche Bahn, the German rail company, the State of Baden-Württemberg, and the City of Stuttgart jointly held a Europe-wide competition for the new station

design. Out of 126 designs submissions, four reached the final round. The winning proposal, by Ingenhoven, Overdiek, Kahlen and Partners (now Ingenhoven, Overdiek, and Partners) was considered by the jury to be the best at integrating the existing station building within a new setting, creating a landmark that, at the same time, responds to the surrounding area of the city. It is conceived as "a sign of forward-looking mobility," which here seems to be not just blind faith in the future, but merging new achievements with old ones. The new station does not claim to mimic the old monumental one; its language of expression tries not to overwhelm, while using an entirely new vocabulary.

The new station concept still keeps the old station hall (1914–27),

built by Paul Bonatz, with its services and its south façade as its point of departure. The most important entrance to the new station, a transparent glass dome, leans directly on it and seems to double its size. The wing additions, however, as well as the train shed with the old tracks, will be torn down. The whole platform area will be built under ground level, turned by an angle of 90 degrees to the old one. The platforms will be spanned by a concrete shell structure, made to be walked on. Four glass domes mark the span of the underneath surface of the station on the ground level and serve as entrances to it. They also delineate the new square, Strassburger Platz. Light is provided through large glass portholes with diameters of 15 meters. These mediate between the

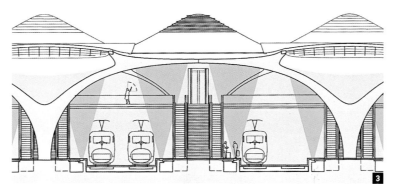

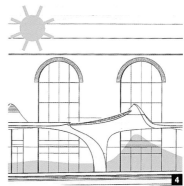

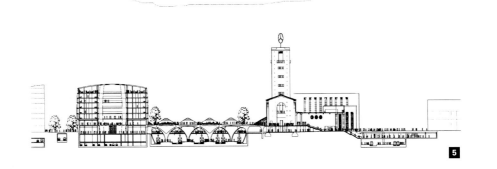

underground area and the square above as well as its surroundings. The new square will eventually become a new focal point in the city. It will serve as a communication space between the main downtown park area (Schlosspark) and the newly developed part. It will also have to fulfill an unusual task of communicating with the station underneath.

A major consideration has been the provision of ecological solutions. Care has been taken not to affect the rich subsoil mineral-water resources. Locating the platforms underground results in a considerable reduction of the noise level of the station activities. By covering the roof with soil, it is expected that the climate inside the station will not exceed 25 degrees Celsius in summer and not fall beneath 14 degrees in winter without additional heating or cooling. The reconstruction will proceed in phases. It is expected that the end of the final phase—the station itself—will be completed by 2008, by which time parts of the surrounding areas will have be completed, too.

5   Transversal section

6   Rendering of platform area

7   Rendering of old station and
    new glass dome

HANAWA STATION AND CIVIC CENTER, HANAWA, JAPAN

Architect: Kuniaki Ito

Engineers: Shigeru Aoki, Yutaka Miwa and Hiroshi Yashiro
Construction completed: 1996

Hanawa, a small town with approximately 12,000 inhabitants, is located in a mountainous area in the south of Fukushima Prefecture. The town forms a mountain resort not far from Tokyo, taking advantage of a large part of the municipal area that is covered with forests and contains a river with plenty of fish. To maintain the natural appearance of the area for tourists attracted by the rural surroundings, leisure facilities, and a hot spring, new constructions in Hanawa must integrate their architecture and nature, and often this is achieved by the use of local materials.

Although it was potentially attractive to visitors, the city, in the late 1980s, faced the problem of a deserted town center, because of migration to the outer districts and an increasing number of commuters. As the small, old railway station in the middle of Hanawa could not meet the requirements of a town's main railway station, citizens demanded a new station building, including civic facilities, to revive the center. In consultation with the residents, a library, a tearoom, and a gallery for exhibitions were chosen as additional facilities to create a new focus for the station and central area.

Kuniaki Ito was commissioned to design the new building. He created six intersecting circular huts with conical roofs connected to two cubic huts with pyramidal roofs. The walls of the whole complex consist of concrete and glass, while the roofs are clad in metal. On the interior, the dark wood of each roof truss is visible and the heavy timber structure resembles a half-opened Japanese umbrella on a circular ring beam. Each hut is supported by either a central column or four columns dividing the loads. The whole building is situated alongside the tracks, though only a small part is actually

1   Plan

2   View of huts along platform

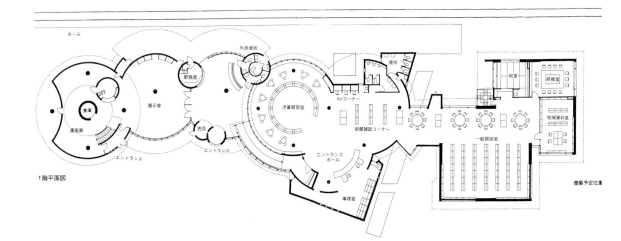

used for station facilities. Much of the space is used for a gallery which is located on one side of the building. On the opposite side of the building is the library, occupying three huts, as well as part of the rectilinear space for book stacks.

Japanese traditional elements are integrated in the building by creating a Tatami room (a room with traditional Japanese mats) in one of the

rectangular rooms of the library and a tearoom located on the second floor, directly under the roof of the gallery hut. Between the gallery and the library can be found a small waiting room adjacent to a shop and ticket office. Canopies, projecting from the roof of the exhibition area and the waiting room, grant protection to the entrance and to the platforms.

Kuniaki Ito's building is not a typical railway station. As with many other new stations, an important requirement in Hanawa was to integrate several functions in one station complex. In contrast to the common approach, the architect seems not to have stressed the building's identity as a railway station. Instead, he has solved the problem by creating an identifiable, unique

building, but one highly integrated with its surroundings. The metal-clad roofs correspond with the mountainous landscape and form a new monument that attracts additional visitors. Both inhabitants and tourists can use new civic facilities in the building in a variety of ways. The influence of the new building on the increased number of visitors has encouraged the refurbishment of Hanawa's main street.

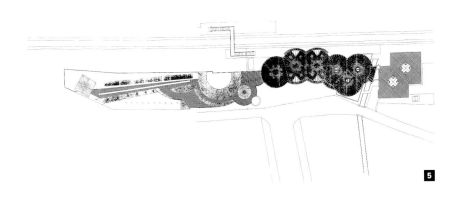

3   Partial view of huts

4   Detail of roof structure

5   Roof plan

6   Partial view of interior of roof

7   Bicycle-parking canopy and view
    away from station

97

KYOTO STATION BUILDING, KYOTO, JAPAN

Architect: Hiroshi Hara

Engineers: Toshihiko Kimura Structural Design Office

Construction completed: 1997

After Japan's national railway company was privatized and split in 1987, Kyoto station became a part of JR West. The station is used by approximately 200,000 passengers daily and serves as a stop for the main Japanese high-speed rail line, the Shinkansen. JR West therefore decided to build a new and larger station building, with facilities for commercial space and cultural activities.

The design of a new station was restricted by several requirements. One important condition relates to its location in Kyoto, a 1200-year-old city with approximately 1,400,000 inhabitants and mainly consisting of three- to six-story buildings. The city is very proud of its many historic houses and temples, as well as the remnants of its ancient street pattern.

As a rich repository of Japanese medieval culture, Kyoto is the destination of more than 40,000,000 national and international tourists annually.

In spite of the fact that only a relatively small site was available, the new station needed to be a large complex, including a department store, leisure activities, and a hotel, to serve the many passengers and tourists who would use it. At the same time, the building's height was limited to 60 meters, in keeping with the city's skyline. The project gave rise to many debates between citizens and planners regarding the influence of such a large-scale building in the townscape. Another JR West-defined goal was to ensure that the railway station function's was evident throughout the whole building, even though the transportation facilities would occupy only a small percentage of the whole space. Finally, the new building was required to form a connection between the adjacent areas of the city to the north and south.

In 1991, Hiroshi Hara won a limited international design competition with a scheme that respected the 60-meter height limit, but created a multifunctional space of

1 View down into concourse

2 South promenade forming a canopy over the platform

3 Central concourse leading to platforms

4 Ground floor plan

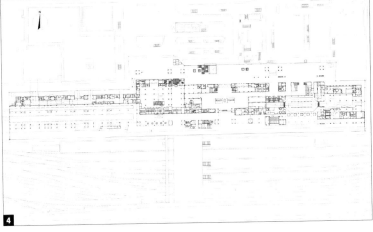

5

5 View along South Promenade

6 Longitudinal section

7 Transversal section

8 Overall view of southern façade

238,000 square meters on the site of 38,076 square meters. The architect designed a 470-meter-long, rectangular building housing the largest commercial development ever made in Kyoto. Express trains to Kansai International Airport, local JR West lines, private railways, buses, and taxis provide a broad spectrum of transportation services located in the new facility. Hara stressed that it was his effort to unite the history of railway and modern architecture in his building.

The station is focused around what is termed "a geographical concourse," a type of atrium that follows a V shape, wider at the top and narrower toward the lower levels. The space is configured by stairways and areas that step back on both sides to form the space. The entrance to the "geographical concourse" is situated on the ground floor. On the west side a grand staircase leads to the sky garden. Located right under the stairs is a department store with a large parking garage, while a café, a hotel lobby, a theater, and several retail facilities occupy the different levels east of the concourse.

Important for tourists is the local government office with passport authority, situated in the southwestern part of the building. Under the 60-meter-high, glazed, double-curved, barrel-vaulted roof, a skyway connects the east and west parts of the building. In the interior, artificial landscapes are created by seventy different kinds of stone, along with bridges, plants, and sculptures. Openings to the outside create a weather-dependent environment in parts of the interior, uniting the outside and inside.

The engineering aspects of the project were especially challenging. The subway tunnels, underground shopping mall, and the below-grade platforms eliminated the possibility of supporting the building with a traditional structure of regularly placed footings and columns. Hiroshi Hara designed an artificial supporting system between the second and third floor, which he calls a "matrix." The dimensions of this structural grid relate to the dimensions of the existing urban fabric in the surrounding area. The matrix can be seen in the promenade projecting over

the first platform, here also serving as an evacuation floor.

Glass is a fundamental material chosen for Kyoto Station. A part of the northern façade is clad with a glazed curtain wall to reflect the sky and thus create a luminous atmosphere on this side of the station. At the lower part of this curtain wall, quadrilateral panes are arranged to create a sky collage, by reflecting the sky at different angles. Triangular panes of glass, visible from the north side, create a dome to shelter the hotel lobby. While the north façade shows the building's division into three parts (station, retail, and hotel lobby), the southern façade consists of a precast-concrete curtain wall, with granite, steel, and aluminum panels, as well as mosaic tiles and reflecting glass. In the center of the long building, views to the south and north are achieved by the large, rectangular opening included on several levels. In an attempt to lessen the mass of the building, as much glass as the budget permitted was used. However, the building is still very powerful in relation to its surroundings.

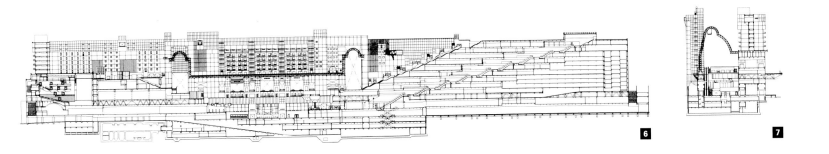

6   7

8

TAZAWAKO STATION AND TOURIST OFFICE, TAZAWAKO-CHO, JAPAN

Architect: Shigeru Ban

Structural Engineers: Gengo Matsui + O.R.S. and JR East Design Corp.

Construction completed: 1997

Tazawako-cho, a small Japanese town with 14,000 inhabitants, is located in the middle of a recreational area in the mountains. Surrounded by woods and adjacent to the beautiful Tazawako Lake, it is a relaxing vacation site for tourists. After the town had been chosen to become a stop along the new Tohoku Shinkansen railway line, architect Shigeru Ban was commissioned to design a new station. The small, old station was absorbed in the new building and transformed into a tourist office.

The architect's primary compositional goal was to guarantee a vista from the station plaza in front of the building through the building and to the mountains behind, as well as allowing open views of arriving and departing trains from inside the building. Also, for arriving passengers a visual link from the platforms to activity in the plaza in front of the building was thought to be useful for orientation.

To provide for these requirements, Shigeru Ban designed a predominantly transparent building on a rectangular ground shape, situated lengthways along the tracks, with a slightly concave, bowed-front façade overlooking the town and the lake. The whole building is constructed on a small podium. Staircases and a ramp for the physically handicapped grant easy access to all users of the entrance area on the south side.

The very limited construction period of seven months called for a design characterized by simplicity. Thus rows of vertical precast-concrete piles on each side, all fixed to the foundation, carry the building's load. Pins connect the top of the pillars to the roof beams, which consist of wood with a steel inlet. A slightly convex curved roof, designed to withstand the local heavy snowfall, shelters the whole space. The rectangular roof creates a large canopy over the rear façade. A secondary canopy is installed directly over the entrance, indicating clearly the point of entry. The interior functions of the station are conceived

1 Overall view of station

2 Staircase leading to second floor

3 View from second floor toward plaza
   in front of station

4 Detail of roof and canopy over entrance

of as independent boxes,
all under the great roof, which allow
easy changes of shape, recalling
traditional Japanese houses.
Additionally, two parts of these roofs
are used as terraces, one in the east
corner to the front, and the other in
the west corner, granting a panoramic
view toward the mountains.

The interior of the building is
characterized by its two functions, as
station and tourist information office.
A foyer, called a communication hall,
occupies the entrance area. It gives

access to a concourse, ticketing
office, and waiting room. In the west
part of the building, the tourist center
can be found. Accessible via a broad
staircase from the concourse, the
second floor houses a cinema club,
an exhibition room, storage space,
and the roof terraces.

KEIHAN UJI STATION, UJI, JAPAN

Architects: Hiroshi Wakabayashi and Keihan Electric Railway Co. Ltd.

Engineers: Building Design Department, Takenaka Corporation

Date completed: 1995

Keihan Uji Station, located in Uji city, which is known for its Byodoin Temple, is a terminal for the Uji line of Keihan Electric Railway. Road expansion and a bridge rebuilding project necessitated a new station. With a roundabout and a public square in front of the station defined in Uji's master plan, the new station had to be more compact than the previous one.

The facility has three zones: the station, an auxiliary building, and the underground connection between the two. The station is also defined by its two distinct sides. The south side is a sightseeing area where the temple and traditional structures exist. To the north is an industrial area with new apartment buildings. The design emerged in response to

these two very different environments, as is symbolized by the two different roof forms employed. The traditional forms are echoed in the repetitive gabled roof line. Toward the south, the bold circles or large vaults cover the concourse of the station.

New stations in Japan reflect a tendency to create buildings that are more than just functional structures.

Currently, they are seen as cultural facilities for town and cities. The architect has stated that he planned this station to represent the "energy of the city and to remain in the memory of the residents as an everlasting landscape."

1   Concourse stairs

2   View of west façade

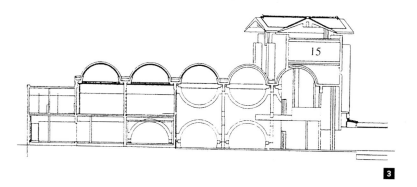

3

4

5 ▶

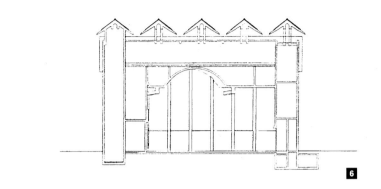

6

7

1

2

3

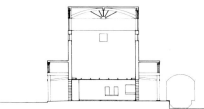

4

5

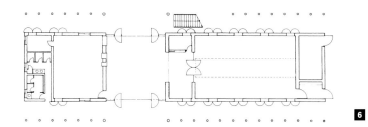

6

YUFUIN RAILWAY STATION, YUFUIN, OITA PREFECTURE, JAPAN

Architect: Arata Isozaki and Associates

Engineers: Mamoru Kawagushi and Engineers and Nippon Kanyo Giken Co. Ltd.

Date completed: 1990

Japan Rail's Yufuin Station stands at the western end of Yufuin, a hot-springs resort town surrounded by lush nature. It is in an area that affords views toward Mount Yufu. A recent increase in the number of tourists demanded the replacement of the existing station, which had become obsolete. For the new facility, the following conditions had to be met: the station was not to be merely a facility for passing through as part of a trip, but should be a forum for visitors and inhabitants to enjoy community culture; it should be a center for information exchange; and it should represent Yufuin symbolically. Furthermore, the building could not exceed a height of 12 meters, in order to comply with town ordinances.

The station uses simple geometry very effectively. It is basically a rectangular building parallel to the tracks, but with an entrance concourse that rises up 12 meters at the center. The cube of the concourse measures 9 meters per side and glass at the top allows light to flow in. The waiting room to one side of the entrance cube was conceived as much as a gallery for exhibitions as a gathering area for travelers. The station offices are located at the opposite side of the concourse.

The entire building is made of wood. Instead of the traditional skeleton system, large glue-laminated assemblies and wood-frame construction were used to create a large space. Small concerts can be given here. The stone-covered floor is heated by using the hot water from the nearby spring. The offices and hall form an open space, constructed by bow-shaped and glue-laminated materials and tension bars. The hall with the top light can also be used as an art gallery by mounting detachable panels on the windows and other openings to create additional display spaces. The outside colonnade offers scenic views of Mount Yufu and the town.

1 Exterior of cupola

2 Interior of cupola

3 Interior of entrance concourse

4 Transversal section

5 Elevation

6 Plan

7 Overall view

MONACO STATION, MONTE CARLO, MONACO

Architects: AREP/Jean-Marie Duthilleul, Etienne Tricaud and Daniel Claris

Engineers: AREP, SNCF Engineering Directorate

Construction completed: 1999

1   Partial view of façade

2   Detail of sun-screening system from the interior

3   Stairs leading from station level to platforms

4   View of platforms

Monaco Station was built as a result of the extension of the high-speed TGV train system to the south of France and the Principality of Monaco. The previous station, which occupied about 4 hectares of precious city land, was torn down and approximately half of the newly won land is destined for new buildings, including commercial, residential, educational, and tourist development, and the other half for public parks and gardens. The location and topography of the new site was the major determining factor and challenge to the design and construction techniques used for the new station. Very little buildable land is available in Monaco. The new station, with its accompanying structures, is built within the very densely populated city on a rocky, sloping site above the sea. It took about six years to build, owing to the need for extensive earth-movement works. The new railway facility consists of a tunnel 2800 meters long with two rail tracks and a flanking platform on each side, the main concourse building with passenger services, and a thirteen-story underground car park. It was built to accommodate approximately 2,000,000 passengers a year.

The most striking feature of the station is the front elevation. Set on the slope, the main entrance is below a great arch that is a roadway viaduct. The arch is filled in with glass-and-marble sunshades that allow natural light to penetrate the station in interesting patterns. From the station entrance there are panoramic views out toward the sea and city. Above the station, and also embedded in the slope, is the parking garage for 700 cars, which also uses an architectural vocabulary of arches. The station is monumental, but not overwhelming, as it is nestled into the cityscape.

The platform area within the tunnel is 430 meters long, 25 meters wide, and 10 meters high. It is a simple concrete structure clad in wood and sound-absorbing concrete panels. These materials, along with careful lighting of the vault, create an almost magical atmosphere. The connection between the two platforms is provided by steel-and-wood overhead walkways, escalators, and glass-enclosed elevators. The main concourse is situated on the level above the tunnel. It provides the usual amenities—ticketing offices, waiting areas, services, and shops—continuing the theme of concrete, wood, and glass. The architects have succeeded in creating an overall harmonious appearance by using few but elegant materials.

AMERSFOORT STATION, THE NETHERLANDS

Architect: Jan van Belkum, Arcadis Architects

Engineers: Arcadis Bouw/Infra
Construction completed: 1997

The impetus for a new station arose because the small Amersfoort station of 1901 could not handle the increasing number of travelers. Although a bank, kiosk, bookstore, and flower shop had been added in several different-shaped annexes over the years, the additions could not solve the problems of the narrow, pedestrian crossings that led to the platforms, especially during the rush hours. A new station building had to be built. As a result of the Dutch government's support for new urban development on station locations, the Amersfoort project led to an ambitious plan to increase the connection between station and town center.

The architect, J.A. van Belkum, was confronted with a task similar to the one he had faced in his design for Hilversum Station. Typically, combinations of office buildings and stations in The Netherlands consisted mostly of an inconspicuous station entrance in an office façade. In response to this, it was decided that the office area should be clearly defined and the entrance to Amersfoort Station should stand out against its surroundings. In van Belkum's design, the station occupies the center of a two-winged building. Office space is provided in the two slightly concave curved wings, which seem to embrace the plaza in front of the station. Situated under an arcade, the stores and cafés on the ground level of the office area offer diversion for waiting travelers, while the east wing connects the building to the town center. The central station hall is framed by two bow-shaped, projecting parts, both supported by large, tapered columns, which signal the main entrance.

Several shades of orange bricks and tiles create a pattern on the façade and divide the building into sections according to its different functions, while the common color orange unites the sections. The brightest orange is used for the projections framing the station hall, thus stressing that part specifically. In contrast to these opaque materials, glass is used for the hall's south-facing wall, which is 20 meters high. Colorful glass installations by the artist Joost van Santen enliven the sunlight entering the space.

The east side of the hall consists entirely of glass and steel. Inside, all the usual station facilities are provided. Adjacent to the rear, the platforms are accessible via a new pedestrian crossing, three times as broad as in the old station. In contrast to its closed predecessor, the new construction makes splendid use of glass, granting a fine view of the old city. An acute-angled glass roof over a horizontal opening in the bent ceiling of the pedestrian crossing allows additional light to reach the interior. The construction of the elevators in the station repeats the acute angle of the roof, indicating the architect's carefully chosen formal language. The station integrates the demand for a visible identity in a high-density area with the requirement to connect the area to the center. In addition, it shows a clear, comprehensible structure, which is a necessity for public-transportation buildings.

1   View of main entrance

2   View just inside main entrance

3   View toward access to platforms

4   Section

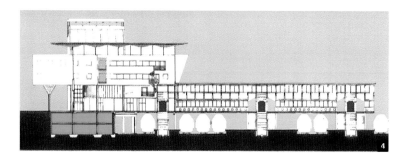

BIJLMERMEER STATION, AMSTERDAM, THE NETHERLANDS

Architects: Nicholas Grimshaw and Partners/Jan van Belkum and Neven Sider, Arcadis Architects

Engineers: Arcadis Bouw/Infra

Estimated completion: 2005

Bijlmermeer, a district in southeast Amsterdam, is an example of the failure of urban planning of the 1960s and 1970s. Built as a satellite town after the precepts of the Athens Charter, the areas for living, working, shopping, and entertainment are strictly separated. The slogan "living in a park" led to a large number of identical-looking eleven-story residential buildings, situated around green spaces and separated by elevated roadways to keep the ground level free of vehicular traffic. The intention was to create the modern city of the future, but instead, a monotonous district was built that was later plagued by high unemployment and a reputation as a poor and unsafe area. As urban-planning strategies try to revive Bijlmermeer and to improve the quality of life of the inhabitants, a new working area with offices, shopping, and leisure facilities has been created. The new station is part of this effort.

The development of a new station in Bijlmermeer was triggered by the planned construction of two new direct tracks between Schiphol Airport and Amsterdam, and two extra tracks to central Amsterdam, along with the overall urban renewal plans. Construction of the new building by Nicholas Grimshaw and Partners began in 2000 and completion is scheduled for 2005. The new construction will be one of the five largest stations in The Netherlands, including a train and metro station with eight tracks (instead of the former four), and an adjacent bus station, serving an estimated total of 60,000 passengers per day.

As the tracks divide the main residential sector from the center, with its shopping malls, cultural facilities, and a famous stadium, a connection between the two areas was required. Elevated tracks are planned, of about 325 meters in length, approximately 9–11 meters above ground and spanning the existing boulevard, 70 meters wide, that connects the different parts of Bijlmermeer. Supported by shopping facilities under the viaduct, this visual link aims to bring the two areas together. Directly beneath the

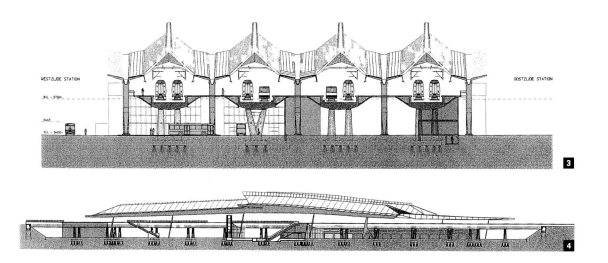

3

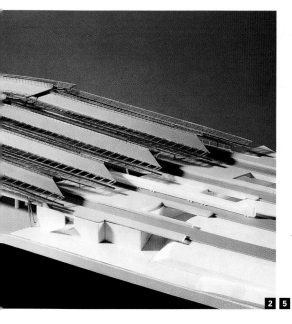

4

boulevard and the tracks will be the station hall, containing a ticket center and retail areas. The 340-meter platforms on the viaduct will be accessible via escalators, stairs, or elevators from the hall.

The most striking feature of the station will be the roof. Each platform will be protected by an identical rib construction, looking like a steel spine, rising toward the center of the station to a height of 6.5 meters and declining at the far ends of the platforms to 3.2 meters. These steel-and-glass elements are extended with

a double-skin metal canopy over the tracks. The longitudinal gaps between the different tracks will be framed with metal elements that protrude upward and look like the fins of a fish. The uplighting from the station will illuminate the vertical openings between the metal elements, creating an impressive glowing image in the darkness. Four A-shaped steel columns will support the roof over each platform, with added stabilization at the bus level. Expressed through the design is the position of the boulevard as indicated in the whole

structure, and emphasized by an opening in the roof, which is created by the overlapping parts.

In addition to the creation of a pleasant atmosphere and a building that is easy to maintain, it was especially important to consider the personal security of the users. The long openings in the platforms allow views to the boulevard and provide daylight under the tracks. Visual contact between the inside and outside of the station is facilitated by the choice of transparent materials.

1   Model, view from street level

2   Model, overall view

3   Transversal section

4   Longitudinal section

5   Perspective of concourse

2 **5**

ARNHEM CENTRAL, THE NETHERLANDS

Architects: Un-Studio/Van Berkel and Bos

Engineers: Arup Associates

Construction: Willems Tunnel, completed. Parking under construction. Transfer Hall expected to be completed 2007

The area around the train station of Arnhem has been the subject of master planning efforts by the innovatory firm headed by Ben van Berkel. While not limited strictly to the design of a train station, the master plan, begun in 1996, creates a new, high-quality public space that is really the main entrance to the town. More than 65,000 visitors pass through the station each day, so it is important symbolically as well as permitting easy connections to other areas of the town.

Three basic entities are involved in the project: the City of Arnhem, Dutch Railways, and ING, a real-estate development company. The architects proposed combining the train station and bus station in a new type of complex: an integrated public-transportation area. The proposal includes a high-rise office tower, new areas for parking, and a large roof covering a major portion of the site. The main aspect of the complex is a climate-controlled inner court that grants direct access to all types of transportation—trains, taxis, buses, cars, bikes, trolleys—as well as to the offices and, subsequently, the town center. The inner court runs easily into the square outside, creating a public urban space for cafés and

restaurants. From this square, the urban landscape transforms into an office-building landscape above the bus station to the west. Bringing together the divergent interests of the three participating entities led to a scheme that links the different functional uses with public spaces, connects the transport station with the city, locates the offices on top of the bus station, and creates a link between the town center and the area north of the station. The final result will include some 55,000 square meters of office space, parking for 1200 cars and 2500 bicycles, and 10,000 square meters of shops and food services.

The naturally sloping site allows transport systems to be brought together in the same building but on two different levels. The architects are creating a new landscape using the concept of "folds" that are determined by natural differences in heights, walking routes, site lines, and the different densities of the uses of the area. The master-planning technique used relies on finding areas of overlapping or shared interests among the different parts. One basic shared element is pedestrian movement. For this reason, extensive studies of movement to and within

the complex were fundamental. The intersection of different traffic systems is reduced to a minimum so that accessibility is maintained. Pedestrians can orient themselves and choose a destination with ease. This clarity of organization is enhanced by the penetration of natural light at key points such as station entrances and the offices.

Because of the scope and complexity of the master plan, it is being undertaken in phases. The tunnel has been completed, the parking facility is under construction, and the transfer hall, offices, and apartments will follow in the coming years.

1 Computer rendering, inside of transfer hall

2 Computer rendering of station, trolley stops, and office towers

3 Computer rendering, detail of station entrance

SANDVIKA STATION, SANDVIKA, NORWAY

Architect: Arne Henriksen

Engineers: Bonde & Co.

Completed: 1994

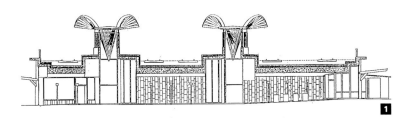

Situated approximately 15 kilometers west of Oslo, Sandvika is within easy commuting distance of the Norwegian capital. Ever since the rail line was built, this little community was cut into two parts. The elevated tracks crossing the town presented a barrier for the development of a unified center. The tall buildings of the old station, built during the boom of the 1960s and 1970s, only increased this division. Efforts in recent years have been directed toward making the

town center more pleasant and hospitable by preserving its historic buildings and converting its main street to a pedestrian walkway. The construction of a new station building was another step in this direction.

The station project both acknowledges the importance that commuting has for this community and supports efforts to make its center open and accessible to both parts of the town. By providing more space for retail shops it also

strengthens the town's small business sector. Architect Henriksen used the elevated position of the tracks and designed the station's main concourse at right angles to them and underneath them, so that it can be entered from the eastern as well as the western side. In this way, the design reconnects the two parts of the town. Flanking the concourse underneath the tracks are the usual railway services and smaller shops. These are set back and so the

walkways become more ample as passengers proceed toward the staircases leading up to the platforms.

The floor and the walls of the concourse are clad in black slate, while the gently arching ceiling is of plain concrete, using a white color similar to the town hall. Large skylights carried by a V-shaped structure made of wood crown the access ways to platforms above. Its repetitive pattern of parallel strips

interspersed with wider elements is reminiscent of railroad ties carrying rails. The skylights, which run perpendicular to the tracks and point the way to the platforms, present a dramatic focal point in the development of the space in the concourse. The use of wood and a similar rhythmic structure create the canopies that protect the platforms. They also help this small station respond to the surrounding forests of evergreens.

The station concourse continues outside the station at street level with an alignment of smaller shops. On the eastern side it closes the square, creating a focal point at the end of the pedestrian zone. On the western side it leads to the bus terminal, which spreads out parallel to the railway tracks and has a car park underneath. Henriksen's station becomes the fulcrum that gives new balance to the center of this community.

1   Section

2   View of station from town square
    in front

3   Partial view of station entrance

4   Platforms

5   Concourse area with stairs
    leading to platforms

6   Detail of structure of skylights

ORIENTE STATION, LISBON, PORTUGAL

Architect: Santiago Calatrava

Engineer: Santiago Calatrava

Construction completed: 1998

Built as a gateway to Expo '98, which commemorated the 500th anniversary of Vasco da Gama's journey to the Indies, this new station for Lisbon was the result of a limited competition. Selected from six competing projects, Santiago Calatrava's proposal was to serve the immediate purpose of the celebration of the world's fair, but also to fulfill far-reaching, longer-term goals. Not only is this station an important interchange between different types of transport—high-speed and standard trains, regional bus lines, metro, tram, and cars (with its park-and-ride facilities)—but it also became the main component and the symbol of the revitalization and transformation of the formerly decaying industrial area of the eastern part of Lisbon called Doca dos Olivais. By 2010, some 25,000 people should be living in the new residential area along the Tagus River, which was once occupied by

military barracks, oil refinery tanks, and industrial facilities.

The station was constructed along the railway tracks that run beside the embankment of the Tagus. It consists of two very dramatic and visible parts: the elevated train station platforms formed by a bridge-like structure raised 11 meters off the ground, 78 meters wide and 260 meters long; and the bus terminal located immediately to the west. The bus station is accessed by a central spine or pedestrian walkway that leads to sweeping glazed canopies that are positioned as ribs along the main axis.

The square on the eastern side of the train station is open toward the original Expo grounds and the future housing area. On this side an arched canopy marks the entrance to the station. The main hall is a connecting square just in the center between the square on the eastern side and the

1 View of platforms with steel-and-glass canopies

2, 3 Station concourse area below elevated tracks

one on the western side. It also offers an easy access to the trains above and the metro below. Below this level there is also underground parking, which, if it were at ground level, would present an obstacle, both visual and physical, for pedestrians. Instead, trees have been planted to create a hospitable setting.

From afar the most visible part of the station is its platform area, which also symbolizes the building's rôle in bringing new life to the area. With its glass-and-steel canopies over platforms looking like palm trees with intertwining branches, the station conveys a picture of an oasis, a fertile zone, that welcomes travelers. With its concealed lighting, it makes a welcoming impression at night, too. As is customary with the work of Calatrava, Oriente Station expresses its strong character through the accentuation of a structural system that creates a powerful image both from a distance and up close.

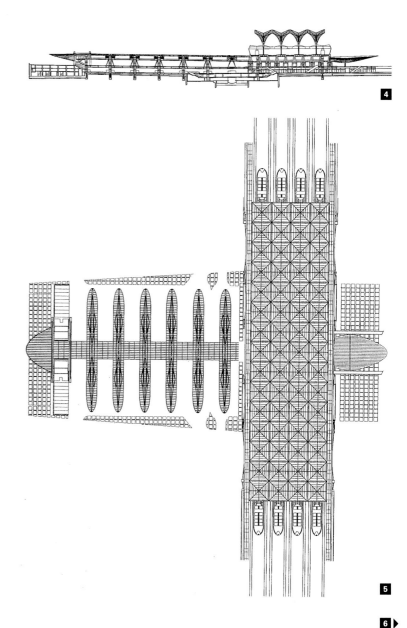

4   Transversal section

5   Roof plan

6   Overall view of station
    with bus stations in foreground

7   Entrance to station and raised
    platforms beyond

PUNGGOL STATION, PUNGGOL, SINGAPORE

Architects: Terry Farrell and Partners

Engineers: Tylin-Singapore

Expected completion: 2001

The station at the new town of Punggol will serve as a significant point of interchange between three rail networks, the Mass Rapid Transit, National Singapore Lines, and Light Rail Transit. The first two of these connect Punggol to the wider transport networks of Singapore, and the third is for intracity transport in the town itself. The station is located at the center of the largest single commercial and residential area as defined by the Punggol city master plan. It is an elongated construction running parallel to the elevated Light Rail Transit lines.

At ground level there is a main road that cuts through the station in an east–west direction. The station reads as a singular metallic gateway, especially when viewed from the main road that runs through the concourse.

Situated to the south of the station is an area zoned for an educational institution and to the north is a residential area organized around a green space. Many design elements reinforce the axial character of the station and relate it to the surrounding zones, such as the landscaping, the retail concessions, and the outdoor seating areas.

Punggol station is planned to be built as the housing in the new town is constructed.

The architect has chosen a long, sweeping curve as the main formal manifestation of the station. The center of the construction is the nucleus of activity and transparency. The floor-to-ceiling glazing on both sides affords dramatic views for passengers and lightens the appearance of the roof covering the whole. At the north and south ends of the station, the vent shafts and cooling towers, contained within a curved metallic enclosure, rise up on

both sides and will frame the future elevated rail lines.

Pedestrian access to the station is located below the architectural fascia, forming a continuous covered route around the concourse perimeter. The transport enclosure of the concourse allows passengers to see directly into the concourse from any point. The ceiling of the concourse is a continuation of the architectural fascia, unifying the interior and exterior of the station. Likewise, the floor treatment is also continuous, with a subtle shift in the use of honed and polished granite.

1　Computer rendering of overall view
of station with roadway through it

2　View at night from street level

3　Earlier scheme, showing segmented roof

4　Final scheme, showing seamless roof

ATOCHA STATION, MADRID, SPAIN

Architect: Rafael Moneo

Engineers: Javier Manterola, ESTEYCO, INECO, Euroestudios
Construction completed: 1992

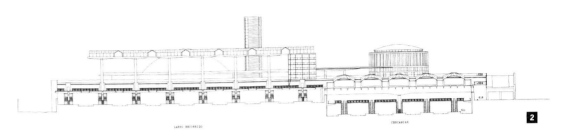

1 Interior of rotunda

2 Transversal section

3 Interior of long-distance train shed

The building of a large, new transportation facility in the center of Madrid posed many complex issues, which architect Rafael Moneo masterfully resolved. The existing terminal of 1892, with its spectacular steel-and-glass shed, had to be preserved, and the new station sited next to it. The old station has become the station hall of the complex, with restaurants, services, and an indoor tropical garden. It is surrounded by a public space, slightly lower than street level, and is accentuated by the new exterior clock tower designed by Moneo. Train service could not be interrupted and therefore

construction had to occur in phases. The site was not flat, but had many different levels. Additionally, the old station faced a roundabout, which was being transformed to eliminate an elevated roadway. The new Atocha Station would also have to contribute to the broader urban context.

The new facility, in addition to providing suburban, long-distance, and high-speed rail services, also connects to a subway station, taxi and bus stops, as well as new parking facilities. The key element in the complex is a rotunda entrance building that can be entered from street level. The brick-and-glass

construction and pure geometry act as a landmark to orient travelers. The building was sited away from the entrance to the old station, easing a potential bottleneck at the roundabout.

After entering the rotunda visitors travel down escalators or stairs to arrive at the commuter train facility with its ten tracks and five platforms. The roof of the commuter station reflects the alignment of the tracks, but also responds to the desire for natural lighting through its skylights and ventilation. Above this part of the complex is one of the parking facilities; it can hold about 670 cars

under dome-like structures interspersed with the projecting skylights.

The new long-distance train shed, defined in part, like the suburban station, by the established pattern of the tracks, has fifteen lines and eight platforms. It was also influenced by its relationship to the old station and the commuter station. The roof, which closely follows the pattern of the tracks, is supported by slender columns, creating a hall of dramatic height. The sides of the building are open, except the north façade, which is transparent and enclosed by a glass wall. Light penetrates the flat griddled roof punctuated by skylights. This simpler, more subtle type of roof was selected in order to be discreet in relation to the old station, and, thus, more compatible.

The architect has used a minimum number of materials in the new station complex: concrete, brick, glass, and accents of cast iron, such as railings and the coverings that wrap the bases of columns. This complex project has been realized through thoughtful strategies for the composition and organization of the whole facility, a respect for the former station building, and an imaginative design solution for the new one.

4   Longitudinal section

5   Platform area for high-speed trains

6   Overall view of station complex

7   Detail of rotunda

8   Parking area

SANTA JUSTA STATION, SEVILLE, SPAIN

Architects: Antonio Cruz and Antonio Ortiz

Engineer: Fernando Martínez Bernabé

Construction completed: 1992

Santa Justa Station was built to coincide with the 1992 international exposition in Seville and to serve a new high-speed rail link between Seville and Madrid. Formerly the journey took about seven hours; now it can be made in less than three. The new building is a substitute for an old station, which was transformed into a cultural facility for exhibitions. Lowering the tracks from ground level to subterranean level, thereby eliminating a barrier between the Guadalquivir River and the city, together with using an undeveloped area, provided a generous site for the new station. The station was the first important construction on the large site. It was conceived as an anchor and a magnet for further urban development. Together with the station, the surrounding three-storey buildings were planned for offices, commercial facilities, and residential spaces. All the buildings are unified by their use of light-colored brick throughout.

The firm of Antonio Cruz and Antonio Ortiz designed a building that is marked by its strong horizontal form. As the station had to be built slightly elevated over the subterranean railway line, it still forms a spacious landmark on the

1   Side elevation

2   Overall view toward main entrance

3   Partial view of train shed
    and platforms

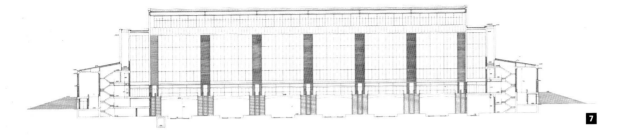

7

open site, resembling a major city terminus, while in reality it is a through station. The architects sought to create a building that is both modern and functional while at the same time urban and monumental.

The station is designed to facilitate easy orientation through its clear organization and by permitting views to its various parts. The traveler approaching the building from the front faces an impressive entrance (14.65 meters above ground), dominated by a slightly curved roof line and a wide, asymmetrically bowed canopy that projects above the large entrance area and provides shelter for arriving and departing passengers. Inside, the terminal has three basic parts: the concourse, a transitional space, and the platforms. In contrast to the rather aerodynamic entrance with its sweeping, curved

canopy, the main concourse building rises up behind it with a rectilinear shape. The façade is formed by a regular row of vertical windows, following the roofline of the entrance building. Clean and even surfaces dominate the interior, with lighting from above adding to the drama of the space. Waiting rooms are situated at the sides of the main hall.

Passing through the great concourse, visitors come upon the transitional space, with stairs and ramps leading down to the platforms. A transparent glass wall separates the concourse from the transitional space, which is clad with bricks. Near the tracks concrete elements are used. The platforms and tracks are sheltered by a roof formed by six single vaults, reminiscent of the architectural vocabulary of traditional stations. To protect the platform area against the

strong summer heat, the bowed steel girders are clad with panels, thereby only allowing light to reach the area through open parts on both sides of each vault and a small gap at the top of each. The vaults are supported by concrete columns that are arranged in a perfectly regular line. An interesting detail is the connection of the vaults cutting into the sloping roof of the transitional space.

To meet the demands of a modern station, the station contains retail areas, but these are carefully placed at the edges of passenger routes, to avoid the impression of a shopping center. Santa Justa Station is an urban monument characterized by a thoughtful, unpretentious design, providing all requirements in a spatially rich setting. In 1992 the design was honored with the Spanish National Architecture Award.

8

◄ **6**

4   View down toward platforms

5   Transitional area from concourse
    down to platforms

6   Main concourse area

7   Transversal section

8   Detail of transitional area

INTERFACE FLON RAILWAY AND BUS STATION, LAUSANNE, SWITZERLAND

Architects: Bernard Tschumi Architects with Luca Merlini Architects

Engineers: Pigetaet Associés, CSD, CSD-Monod

Construction completed: 2000

1 Overall view showing pedestrian bridge, circulation tower, and entrance leading to below-ground facilities

2 Detail of circulation tower

3 View at night from street level

The design for this public-transportation station of 18,600 square metres provides a connection for bus routes, suburban rail lines, and the subway system of Lausanne. The proposal is the result of a two-stage competition held in 1989. Bernard Tschumi Architects was one of three firms that progressed to the second phase of the competition. Tschumi's proposal for a "bridge-city" scheme was selected to be developed by the city of Lausanne in 1991. It proposes a series of four "inhabited bridges" to augment Lausanne's existing system of bridges, so necessary in this city of topographic extremes. The bridges create a new density of spatial relationships and uses. They are both vertical and horizontal connectors linking the lower levels of the valley to the higher, historic city.

The first bridge connects the Flon Valley with the older, outlying neighborhoods and serves as an intermodal transport facility. The station also incorporates public spaces, along with office and retail

facilities, and permits pedestrian traffic on multiple levels.

The four-level structure extends approximately 180 meters across the valley. It is composed of two basic parts: the western end, which is devoted to office and commercial space; and the eastern end, which allows vertical circulation via stairs, escalators and elevators. The architects talk of the western part as being conceived as an enormous hollow-steel beam that stabilizes the bridge. The commercial space at the second level is suspended from the top of the beam and a continuous steel trellis encloses the structure.

To the east, a glass box contains the vertical-circulation routes that connect the underground train platforms, the bus stop, and the offices above. A café will also be included. Along the length of the eastern section of the structure is a "media strip," an automated advertising space that is visible both from the interior of the bridge and at a distance.

CHANNEL TUNNEL TERMINAL, FOLKESTONE, KENT, UNITED KINGDOM

Architect: Building Design Partnership

Engineers: Building Design Partnership

Construction completed: 1994

The Channel Tunnel Terminal, located near Folkestone, is not a traditional railway station: it was specifically designed to serve motorized passengers and their vehicles on double-deck trains on their way to and from France. It can be thought of as a shuttle system connecting Folkestone and Calais, a ride of just over half an hour. The service uses two train tracks and a loop at each end. By connecting road and rail systems the new facility is a hybrid structure, rather like a highway service station laid out in a form of an air terminal. The brief called for a terminal that could handle 785 cars, 74 buses, and 130 trucks an hour. Building Design Partnership (BDP) began preliminary work on this project as early as 1971. Over the years it was stalled owing to lack of British government support, but it was eventually completed in 1994.

The designers were confronted with a site within a rural landscape that is 5 kilometers long and only 750 meters wide. The area, formally designated as being of Outstanding Natural Beauty, had to be protected in the highest degree possible. The task was to funnel the traffic efficiently through tollbooths, a service center, and border controls to the embarkation center, while keeping the new architecture as low-key as possible. BDP delineated the site by the motorway and the loop and built nineteen smaller buildings within it. The terminal complex is partially screened, both visually and acoustically, through a landscape design that includes the creation of berms and a massive program of new plantings that involved the reuse of excavated soil from the site. Great attention was paid to the height of the new architecture so that none of the buildings would overwhelm the surrounding natural landscape. The new constructions used relatively few materials: steel, concrete, aluminum sheeting, and glass. The predominant color is white, with secondary colors of silver and gray. None of the buildings exceeds four stories, the control tower being the only one that reaches that height. Public buildings are characterized by their openness through the extensive use of glass.

Only the buildings housing services not accessible to the public are closed concrete structures.

If the tallest building of the complex is the control center, the centerpiece is the amenity center, with shops, restaurants, and restrooms. This is a three-story cube with a translucent fabric roof that rises up like a tent and is supported by a tensile structure. At night the roof is lit from inside, and thus transformed into a beacon. The front elevation continues the nautical theme by making a reference to the ships in the nearby harbor.

A geometrical pattern is imposed on the site by the routes that lead the traffic (passenger and freight separately), parking spaces, and the queuing lanes leading to the embarkation platforms. At the far end of the site there is a simple portal of the tunnel, the point where the train disappears underground. The sensitive design, expressing concern for the ecology of the setting, has led to a solution that seeks to create a national monument without being monumental.

1   Aerial view of site at Cheriton, near Folkestone

2   Passenger terminal building

3   Control center

4   Freight-scanning building with a lightweight, glazed shed

5   Passenger terminal with fabric roof illuminated at night

STRATFORD REGIONAL STATION, LONDON, UNITED KINGDOM

Architect: Wilkinson Eyre Architects Ltd.
Engineers: Hyder Consultant Ltd.
Construction completed: 1999

In July 1994 Chris Wilkinson was the winner of a limited design competition for a new station building in Stratford, east London. As the construction of a new station formed an important part of an urban-redevelopment project, special attention had to be paid to the effect of the design on the area. Four different railway lines cut through the site: the North London line and London Underground's Jubilee line run roughly north–south while the Underground's Central line and an overground line cross the North London line in a southwest–northeast direction. Another limiting factor, Channelsea River, runs underneath part of the construction site.

Two main tasks of the design were to reunite the split area and to guarantee an easy access to four different railway lines. As replacement for the old subterranean station, Wilkinson created a large building above ground, providing one station for all four lines. On a rectangular ground shape, the complex is situated lengthways alongside the elevated tracks of the Central and overground lines, with the North London line running straight through the building and the Jubilee line terminating in the western part of Stratford Station.

Between the building's rear and the southwest–northeast-running railway lines, space for a planned future line is left. Adjacent to the train facilities is a new bus station and a new drop-off point for cars and taxis.

The most impressive feature of the station is the quarter-elliptical roof, rising from the upper walkway at the back of the building and sheltering the huge concourse. Constructed of tapered, bowed steel girders placed in a row, supporting a silvery shining aluminum cladding, the roof provides a landmark for the whole area. At the front, each steel girder is supported by an inclined steel pillar; four enormous reinforced-concrete piers, carrying the building loads, are positioned between the tracks and the river. Both end walls and the lower part of

2

1 View south toward Jubilee line platforms

2 Dissected axonometric

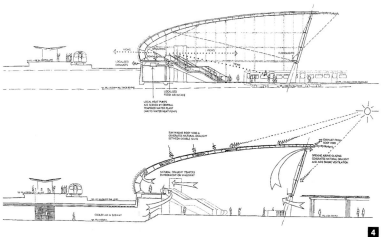

the roof consist of glazing. The effect is a highly transparent building that permits daylight to penetrate the interior and forms a visual link between the inside and the surrounding area. To illuminate the interior at night, high-energy uplights have been installed under the aluminum cladding, accompanied by softer downlights, providing an inviting atmosphere.

Additionally, the roof is designed to allow solar-energy-assisted ventilation, by using the chimney principle. Through a void to the concourse at the lower part of the roof, hot air streams in the space between the double skin, and is exhausted through an opening at the highest part of the ellipse. Thus circulation and comfortable temperatures on hot days inside the building are guaranteed.

Orientation between the potentially confusing railway lines is facilitated by the large open space of the concourse, which is divided into two parts by the North London line. The two parts are connected by a walkway at the rear part of the hall, accessible via glazed elevators and stairs. The space under the walkway is intended to serve as retail spaces and cafés.

The building integrates station requirements for four railway lines, while the highly visible roof creates a focus for the area. Commercial development is planned north and east of the railway complex. To link the site to Stratford center, landscape with artwork has been created around the building, at the same time giving the town a new recreation zone.

3   View from west

4   Principles of illumination and cooling

5   Concourse area leading to platforms

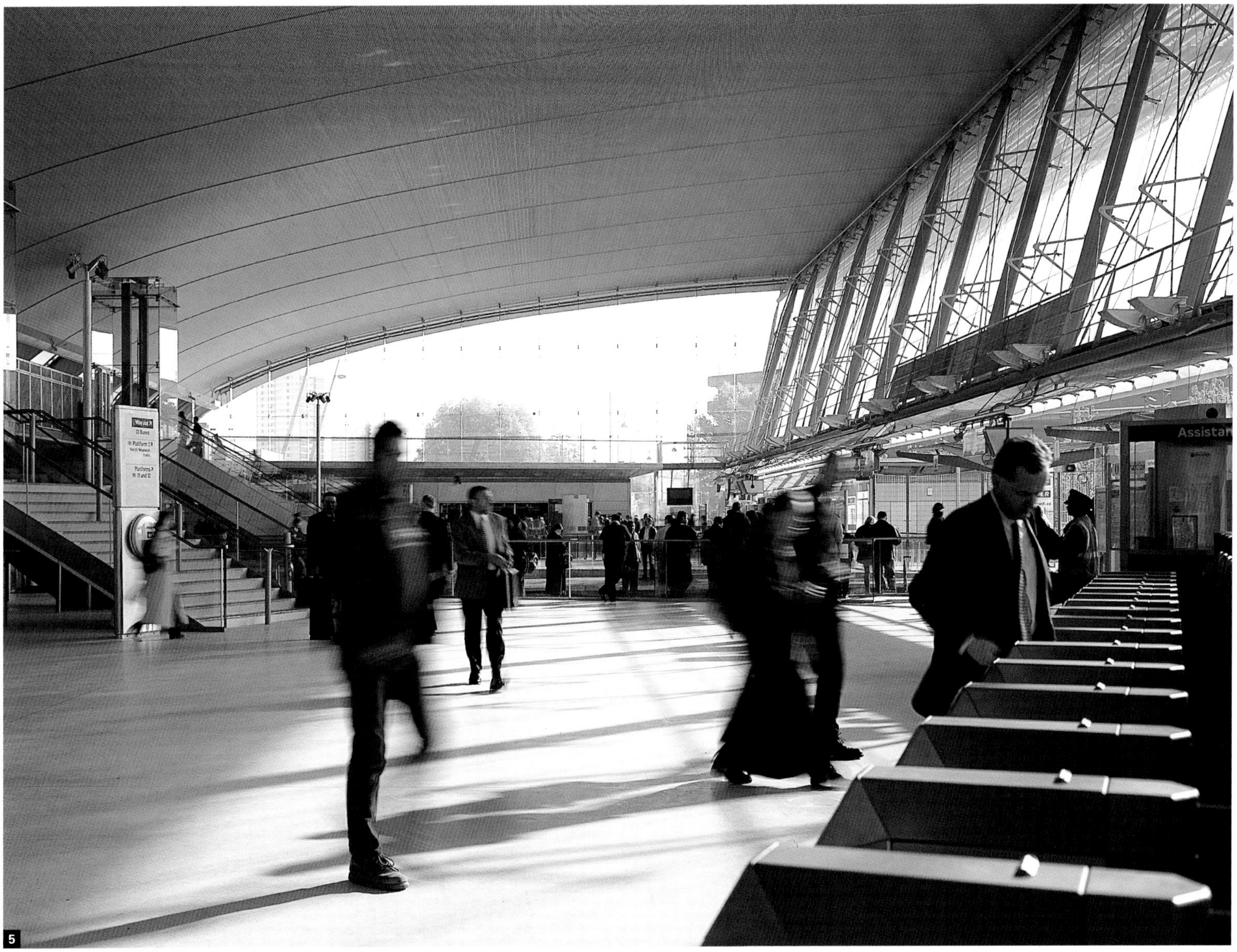

5

PENNSYLVANIA STATION REDEVELOPMENT PROJECT
NEW YORK CITY, NEW YORK, U.S.A.

Architects: Skidmore, Owings & Merrill LLP, David C. Childs and Marilyn Taylor, Partners-in-charge

Engineers: Arup, Parson Brinkerhoff Quade and Douglas

Estimated completion: 2005

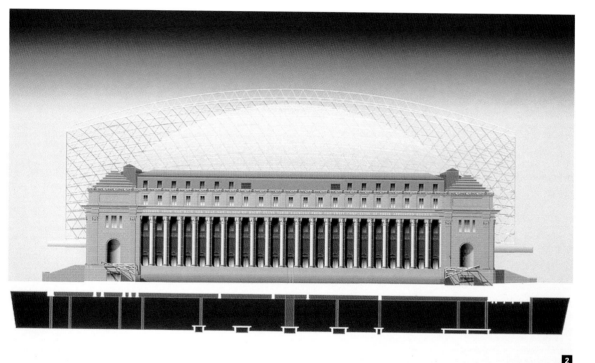

Penn Station will be created anew through the use of the Farley Post Office Building, designed by McKim, Mead and White and constructed in 1914, situated one block west of the current underground Penn Station beneath Madison Square Garden. The aim of the redevelopment project is not simply to convert the Farley Post Office into a copy of the old Penn Station. Rather, the plan is to integrate the great scale of the building and its Neo-classical details with the latest information and circulation technologies and elements of contemporary architecture.

This repositioning of one of New York City's major gateways, which serves over 500,000 passengers daily, will serve as a catalyst for new utilization of the North Chelsea area. The new train station will form a continuous economic corridor between the Times Square area and recently improved West Chelsea. In order to accommodate the new 31st and 33rd Street entrances, the existing moat running parallel to the post office on the northeast and southeast corners and along the north and south sides will be filled in, thus widening the street and offering surface access. Current truck traffic will be diverted to underground service ramps that will not only improve traffic circulation but also

1   Rendering of glass crescent
    at 33rd Street entrance

2   Section showing lower level,
    façade of Farley Post Office Building
    and glass crescent

3   Rendering of interior
    of 33rd Street entrance

3 ▶

POST OFFICE

AMTRAK

4 5

6

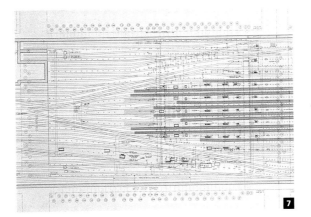

7

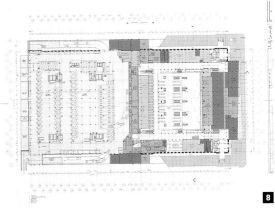

8

4   Dissected axonometric showing post-office and Amtrak/retail facilities

5   The crescent geometry in plan

6   Rendering of aerial view

7   Platform plan

8   Concourse plan

9   Rendering of platform area with skylit train hall above

make the area far more inviting for automobiles and pedestrians.

The redevelopment will focus on the area between the original post office and its 1935 extension. This space will be converted to a great concourse that will contain the western façade of the 1914 building. An immense glass-and-nickel trussed skylight extending 46 meters upward will cover the main (33rd Street) entrance and the hall's ticketing and check-in facilities. This spectacular glass crescent, derived from a section of a sphere, will evoke the old Penn Station's physical stature in this great point of arrival.

The train hall and waiting area is to be constructed in the skylit courtyard of the 1914 post office, which once served as a mail sorting room. Passengers will wait for trains beneath historic, wedge-shaped trusses, where incoming trains will be visible through

the floor. A media wall will provide entertainment and information such as arrivals and departures, weather, and financial news. Three levels of retail space, totaling about 4650 square meters, will surround the train concourse and serve commuters with restaurants and services.

The redeveloped Penn Station will house terminals for Amtrak, including the hub for the new high-speed train, the Acela Express, which serves the Northeast Corridor. Also, the station will provide future rail links to Newark, La Guardia, and John F. Kennedy airports. The United States Postal Service will maintain its operations in the Farley Post Office, keeping 93,000 square meters, including the entire 1935 annex, office space in the 1914 building, and the 8th Avenue lobby, with its monumental stepped entrance.

9

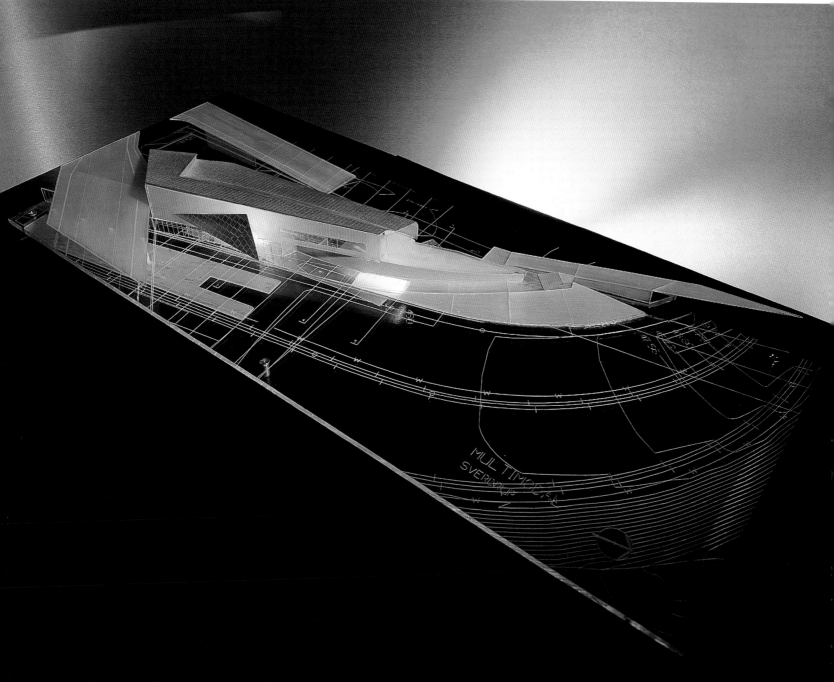

ST. LOUIS GATEWAY TRANSPORTATION CENTER, MISSOURI, U.S.A.

Architects: Adrian Luchini, Jacobs Facilities Inc., Michael E. Kennedy, Kennedy Associates

Engineers: Sverdrup Civil, Inc.
Estimated completion: 2004

1 Section, train and bus station

2 Model, metro station

3 Rendering of entrance area
  for metro station

The planned multimodal transit center consists of two buildings, one containing the Amtrak and Greyhound bus station, the other occupied by a Metrolink stop. Situated in an area of heavy traffic next to railroad lines and on two different sides of an elevated highway, the two buildings will be linked by an enclosed pedestrian walkway, which will provide a safe and weatherproof connection.

Architect Adrian Luchini, of the St. Louis office of the firm Jacobs (formerly Sverdrup), designed an asymmetrical Metro complex of 1300 square meters, to expand the old Kiel Civic Center Station. Situated at the northern edge of an urban site, this

building affords exceptional views of downtown St. Louis. It can be seen from the elevated highway as well as from the access ramp leading on to the westward causeway. The building is exposed significantly to either the car or pedestrian traffic. Its footprint is informed by the motion of the traffic flow and its section by the five different levels that must be connected inside. Its two fundamental components, the eastern façade and the roof, respond to the complex urban conditions previously mentioned. The east façade, perceived from the Metro platforms, the Kiel Auditorium, and the westbound vehicular ramp, will have the role of a

"gate" into this complex. By appearing as a vertical single plane made of glass and extruded-polycarbonate panels, it will glow at night, becoming a true marker for the site. The roof, conceived as a single plane, made of metal panels, curves on to the west side, becoming the west façade. At the north edge, a terrace overlooking downtown follows the pedestrian ramp towards 15th Street and the Kiel Auditorium. To the south, the building becomes a concourse linkage with the new Amtrak and Greyhound terminal. Owing to its position on the site, this building will have two façades only— one fast and the other slow; one vertical and the other horizontal—but

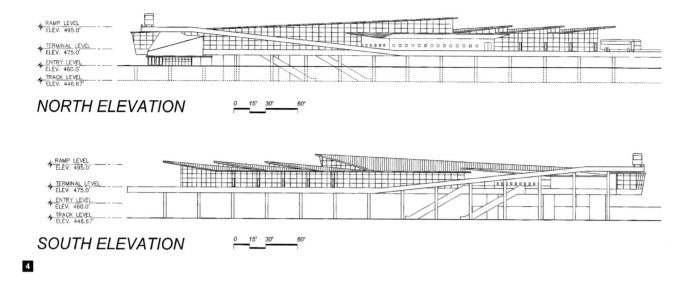

RAMP LEVEL
ELEV. 495.0'

TERMINAL LEVEL
ELEV. 475.0'

ENTRY LEVEL
ELEV. 460.0'

TRACK LEVEL
ELEV. 446.67'

NORTH ELEVATION 0 15' 30' 60'

RAMP LEVEL
ELEV. 495.0'

TERMINAL LEVEL
ELEV. 475.0'

ENTRY LEVEL
ELEV. 460.0'

TRACK LEVEL
ELEV. 446.67'

SOUTH ELEVATION 0 15' 30' 60'

4

many roles, users, and identities.

The expanded Kiel Civic Center Station will include a concourse of 465 square meters at track level on the west side, housing ticket offices for Metro, Bi-state Bus, airlines, and rental-car services. Retail is intended to spread on the east side of the first floor and in the second level of the extension, together with a planned restaurant in the upper level, overlooking the future triangle of green space in front of the station. Local railroads on the east side will be expanded by adding a platform and tracks to store trains, helping to improve transport before and after Kiel Civic Center events. To provide the building's accessibility, an adjacent elevated street will be extended, also giving space for a city bus station, which is linked to the ground floor by stairways inside the station building. Parking space near the transport center for 150 cars supports an easy change between car and train.

The connection to the Amtrak and Greyhound Station building is formed by a pedestrian walkway from the Metro center's concourse. Located south of Highway I-64, the 2230-square-meter building is elevated over the Amtrak tracks. This component of the complex is designed by the St. Louis firm of Kennedy Associates. The two-level building is seen as a horizontal structure raised up over the train tracks. Platforms can be accessed by stairs or elevators. On the west side at entry level, a large square provides space for ten buses at slips and six at one time in a holding area on the bus deck. Providing a direct connection to the bus stops, the building is accessible via doors from the square leading to a waiting lounge shared by Amtrak and Greyhound passengers. The offices and ticketing facilities for bus and train travel flank the central waiting lounges. A taxi stand and a drop-off area are located under the elevated building near the tracks, to facilitate the traffic flow outside and adjacent to the station.

Transparent glazed walls comprise the bulk of the public spaces, affording views to the city and train yards. The station overlooks the tracks below, providing a heightened awareness of the travel experience and reinforcing the sense of movement.

4 Train and bus station, north and south elevations

5 Train and bus station, terminal level plan

6 Overall view of site with train and bus station to left and metro station in center foreground

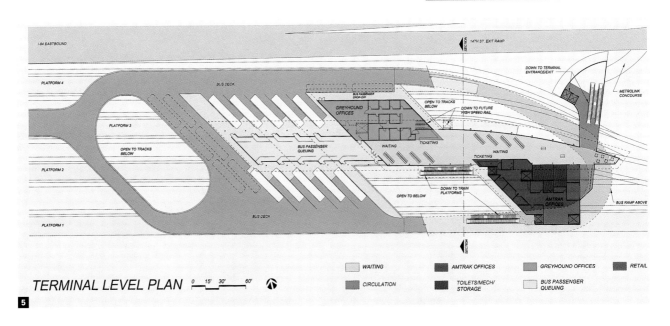

TERMINAL LEVEL PLAN 0 15' 30' 60'

| | WAITING | | AMTRAK OFFICES | | GREYHOUND OFFICES | | RETAIL |
| | CIRCULATION | | TOILETS/MECH/STORAGE | | BUS PASSENGER QUEUING | | |

5

St. Louis Transportation Center

6

149

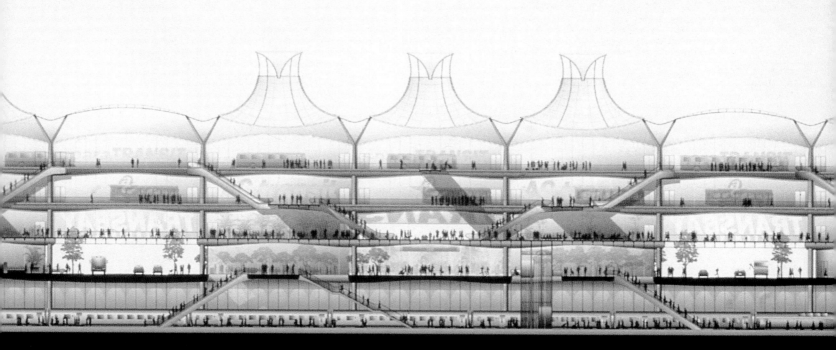

TRANSBAY TERMINAL SAN FRANCISCO, CALIFORNIA, U.S.A.

Architects: SMWM and Richard Rogers Partnership

Engineers: Arup

Estimated completion: 2008

A multimodal transit facility of 55,750 square meters is proposed to meet the increasing travel demands of the San Francisco Bay region and the state of California. It is being planned as an environmentally sustainable design that will facilitate travel and connections for bus and rail passengers using services provided by several transit systems. Located in downtown San Francisco, the terminal will serve as a link between trains on the Caltrain Peninsula lines, when these are extended to the new terminal, and trains serving the East Bay. The new facility will also provide links to other cities via conventional rail services and an eventual high-speed rail line between San Francisco and Los Angeles and other points. The bus component, another significant part of the station, has fifty bays on two levels, to accommodate up to 35,000 daily bus passengers.

The lead planning team has stated that the new building should be designed to encourage and accommodate new transit ridership while also being a memorable public structure—a celebratory building that is an appropriate gateway to and from San Francisco. A plan for new high-

1   Rendering of partial section

2   Rendering of terminal at night

3   Section indicating streets in relation to terminal

4   Area plan showing location of terminal

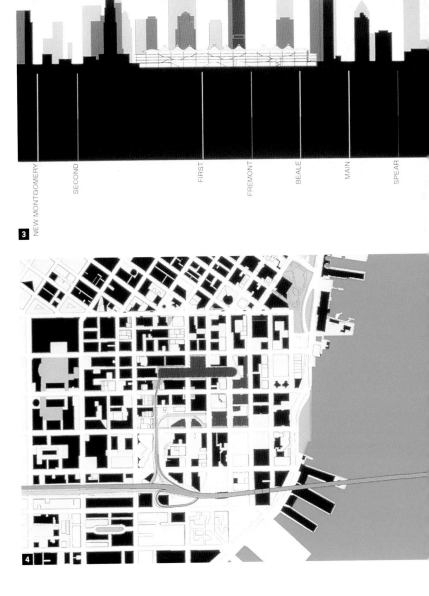

rise, mixed-income housing in the surrounding neighborhood, along with the potential for new offices, a hotel and conference center, educational facilities, and retail outlets, seeks to address broader development goals for the area.

The proposed design is a five-level facility, 400 meters long and 50 meters wide, with a structural framing system that permits unimpeded vehicular and pedestrian movement both horizontally and vertically. Well-distributed access points permit people to enter, pass through, and exit the facility at multiple locations along the street and second-floor concourse level.

One subterranean level is planned for train service. The street level includes the lobby for Greyhound bus routes and accommodates MUNI buses and trolley coaches. The next level up is the concourse level, with all the usual services for ticketing, dining, and shopping. The upper two levels are programmed for commuter buses and Greyhound and other private bus operators. Significant sustainable design features include optimizing natural ventilation by harnessing the reliable prevailing winds, designing the roof and exterior walls to maximize natural lighting, and capturing rainwater for maintenance and irrigation.

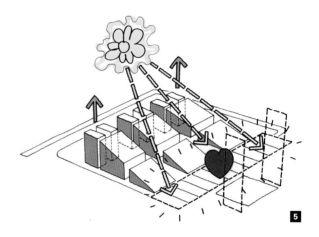

5

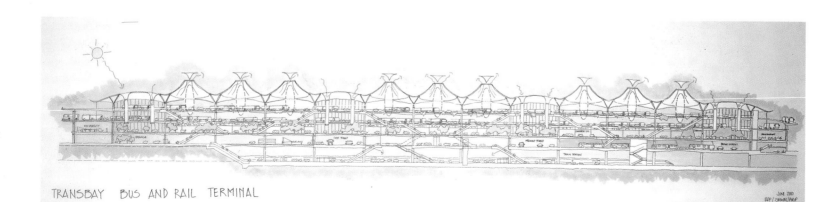

TRANSBAY BUS AND RAIL TERMINAL

6

5   Conceptual diagram for permitting
    sunlight to reach terminal

6   Longitudinal section

7   Site model

8   Computer rendering
    of building cutaway

9   Model, partial view of interior

SOLANA BEACH STATION, CALIFORNIA, U.S.A.

Architect: Rob Wellington Quigley

Structural Engineers: Integrated Structural Design

Construction completed: 1995

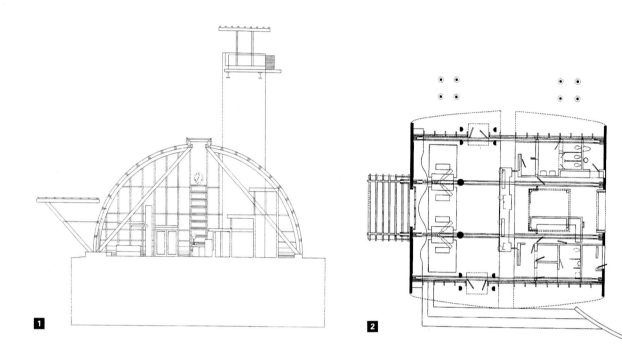

1 **2**

The construction of a new railroad station in Solana Beach was the first part of a $20,000,000 urban-planning project intending to create a new center on a site of 35,000 square meters. Retail facilities, restaurants, movie theaters, low-cost housing, artists' lofts, and a large parking garage are part of the complex, located north of the station. An important requirement for the development on this site was a unique but appropriate design, fitting for this particular city. In connection with the new station, a further task was the elimination of railroad crossings in the area, in an effort to improve the traffic flow, especially on Highway 101.

Rob Wellington Quigley was chosen for the project, not only because of his architecture, but also because of his democratic design process and concern for public participation. To integrate local citizens in the creation of a new town center, the city council initiated workshops for local community groups, giving inhabitants the chance to make proposals concerning the scale, traffic flow, acoustic isolation, and the relationship between commercial buildings and housing areas. In several meetings, the architect presented his ideas, and developed plans in concert with the citizens' requests. From this

cooperation, a design for the new station emerged.

The final shape is based on the Quonset hut—dating from 1940–45, these semicircular buildings are common in the area—and regional greenhouses. Situated in the midst of a small palm grove, the station building consists of a barrel-vaulted construction, with pre-weathered zinc cladding on the vaulted part and large glass windows with vertical steel mullions on the east and west façades. A steel-and-wood canopy on the south side protects a large window in the wall. The architect combines passive, energy-conscious design elements in forming the

1 Section

2 Plan

3 Overall view of platform side at night

3 ▶

shaded south façade and allowing generous cross-ventilation with added air conditioning. Inspired by European railroad architecture, a round clock is centered in each of the main glass façades.

One of the features, developed in the community meetings, is the 21-meter-high, white-concrete tower, with a wood-and-steel top, growing out of the station hall. Because the town had no landmark, the citizens demanded the creation of a visible symbol, which would also emphasize the project's urban importance. To legalize the tower's construction, the council granted a zoning exception to the normal 10.7-meter height limit in Solana Beach. This part of the building, however, is not open to the public, because of the lack of access for the handicapped.

The tracks are located to the west of the concourse, lowered in a 7.5-meter-deep depression to prevent traffic disturbance at grade crossings. To get to the platforms, passengers have to traverse a small terraced distance via stairways or a ramp. Inside the building is the station hall, the entrance not centered under the clock, as one would expect, but moved toward the south. A redwood-paneled ceiling creates a pleasant

8

natural atmosphere. The asphalt-tiled floor stresses the thoroughfare character of the building and its skylight divides the semicircular roof. Beyond the long ticket counter is a waiting lounge with benches made of precast concrete and rubber inserts.

SELECTED BIBLIOGRAPHY

James Abbott (ed.), *Jane's World Railways*, 39th edn, Coulsdon, Surrey (Jane's Information Group) 1997

Geoffrey Freeman Allen, *Railways of the Twentieth Century*, New York (W.W. Norton) 1983

—— *Railways Past, Present and Future*, London (Orbis Publishers) 1982

Francisco Asensio Cerver, *The Architecture of Stations and Terminals*, New York (Arco) 1997

Ira J. Bach and Susan Wolfson, *A Guide to Chicago's Train Stations: Present and Past*, Athens OH (Ohio University Press/Swallow Press) 1986

Brigitte Beil and Alexander Neumeister, *Design for High-Speed Transport of Tomorrow—Projects by Neumeister Design, Munich*, Stuttgart (Design Center) 198674.5

Leo van den Berg and Peter Pol, *The European High-Speed Train and Urban Development: Experiences in Fourteen European Urban Regions*, Brookfield VT (Ashgate Publishing) 1998

Marcus Binney, *Architecture of Rail: The Way Ahead*, London (Academy Editions) 1995

—— *Great Railway Stations of Europe*, photographs by Manfred Hamm, London (Thames and Hudson) 1984

Alex Buck (ed.), *Alexander Neumeister.*
Designer Monographs 8. Frankfurt (Verlag Form) 1999

Gordon A. Buck, *A Pictorial Survey of Railway Stations*, Somerset (Oxford Publishing) 1992

Peter Burman and Michael Stratton (eds.), *Conserving the Railway Heritage*, London (E. & F.N. Spon) 1997

Carl. W. Condit, *Bibliography of the Design, Construction, and Operation of Railroad Passenger Stations, 1875 to date*, Crete NB (J.B. Publishing) 1979

Michael J. Del Vecchio, *Railroads across America: A Celebration of 150 Years of Railroading*, Osceola WI (Motorbooks International) 1998

C. Douma, *Stationsarchitectuur in Nederland, 1938–1998*, Zutphen (Walburg Press) 1998

Brian Edwards, *The Modern Station: New Approaches to Railway Architecture*, London (E. & F.N. Spon) 1997

Espace Croisé (ed.), *Eurolille: The Making of a New City Center*, trans. Sarah Parsons, Basel (Birkhäuser) 1996

Meinhard von Gerkan, *Renaissance of the Railway Station: The City in the 21st Century*, Braunschweig/Wiesbaden (Friech, Vieweg & Sohn) 1996

Siegfried Giedion, *Die Herrschaft der Mechanisierung*, Hamburg (Europäische Verlagsanstalt) 1994

Stephen B. Goddard, *Getting There: The Epic Struggle between Road and Rail in the American Century*, Chicago (University of Chicago Press) 1996

H. Roger Grant and Charles W. Bohi, *The Country Railroad Station in America*, Boulder CO (Pruett Publishing) 1978

Lawrence Grow, *Waiting for the 5:05: Terminal, Station, and Depot in America*, New York (Main Street/Universe Books) 1977

Klaus Heinrich and Rolf Kretschmar (eds.), *Transrapid MagLev System*, Darmstadt (Hestra-Verlag) 1989

Alan A. Jackson, *The Railway Dictionary: An A–Z of Railway Terminology*, Stroud, Gloucestershire (Alan Sutton Publishing) 1992

Philip Jodidio, *Estacao do Oriente*, Lisbon (Centralivros) 1998

Martine Lobjoy, *Roger Tallon, Designer Industriel: De la TV aux TGV*, Paris (Centre Georges Pompidou) 1995

David Wharton Lloyd and Donald Insall, *Railway Station Architecture*, rev. edn, North Pomfret VT (David and Charles) 1978

Carroll Louis Vanderslice Meeks, *The Railroad Station: An Architectural History*, New Haven CT (Yale University Press) 1956; reprinted New York (Dover Publications) 1995

Jens Nielsen, *DSB Design, Danish Railway Design*, Copenhagen (Danish Design Council) 1984

Steven Parissien, *Station to Station*, London (Phaidon) 1997

Jeffery Richards and John M. MacKenzie, *The Railway Station: A Social History*, Oxford (Oxford University Press) 1986

Julian Ross (ed.), *Railway Stations: Planning, Design and Management*, Oxford (Architectural Press) 2000

Jack W. Seto, *Railroad Stations in the United States*, Monticello, IL (Council of Planning Librarians) 1978

Mitchell P. Strohl, *Europe's High Speed Trains: A Study in Geo-Economics*, Westport CT (Praeger Publishing) 1993

Minoru Takeyama, *Transportation Facilities: New Concepts in Architecture and Design*, trans. Hiroshi Watanabe, Tokyo (Meisei Publications) 1997

Joseph Vranich, *Supertrains: Solutions to America's Transportation Gridlock*, New York (St. Martin's Press) 1993

Chris Wilkinson, *Supersheds: The Architecture of Long-Span, Large-Volume Buildings*, Oxford (Butterworth-Heinemann) 1991

John H. White, Jr., *The American Railroad Passenger Car*, Baltimore MD (Johns Hopkins University Press) 1978

ACKNOWLEDGMENTS

The efforts required to bring to fruition this publication, and the exhibition it accompanies, have been substantial and reflect the contributions of many individuals to whom I am indeed grateful. Many have given their advice, energy, ideas, and time to this project, and they deserve more thanks than can be conveyed in these brief words.

The project began within the Department of Architecture at The Art Institute of Chicago as a chance to view some of the many facets of the complex task of designing for rail transportation. Thus, my thanks go first to my colleagues within the department, who provided enthusiasm and assistance every step of the way. Research on the individual stations discussed in this book was begun by Annemarie van Roussel and diligently continued by Lawrence Ebelle-Ebanda, Emily Pugh, Simone Neuhaeuser, Monika Pemic, and Almut Grypstra.

The authors, who have so carefully undertaken their texts, deserve particular recognition for thoughtfully commenting on the current state of train design, as analyzed by Claudia Wessner, and the possible future for train travel in the United States, as examined by Don Phillips.

A special word of appreciation is due to Julian Honer, Maggi Smith, and Matt Hervey of Merrell Publishers, London, and to Amanda Freymann and Robert V. Sharp of the Publications Department at The Art Institute of Chicago for their care in editing, designing, and producing this volume. Likewise, the many photographers who have captured the beauty of the projects reflected here also deserve recognition.

Sincere thanks are in order for the architects, designers, manufacturers, and allied companies and the many people in their firms who have contributed to this book and its accompanying exhibition by providing the necessary documents and materials related to their work. They are the true protagonists of this project. It would be impossible to list all those who have responded to the call for assistance and advice, but special mention goes to Nicholas Grimshaw, not only for his words of wisdom, but also for his inspiring architecture, as well as to Kevin Brubaker, Mike Loundes, Harriet Parcells, Dominique Paultre, J.P. Ruiz, Ellen Taylor, and Cesar Vergara.

For the exhibition at The Art Institute of Chicago, I want to express my thanks and appreciation to partners David Childs and Marilyn Taylor of Skidmore Owings & Merrill LLP in New York, who, along with a number of their collaborators in both New York and Chicago, have created an inspiring installation. Many departments within the museum—Art Installation, Development, Director's Office, Graphics, Imaging, Museum Registration, Physical Plant, Public Affairs, and Publications—have also contributed their services in a most professional way, and they are commended for their dedication and the high standards with which they approach each project. In particular, I wish to acknowledge David Ciske, Cesar Citraro, Phil Kennedy, Lisa Key, William Heye, John Hindman, Martha Sharma, Anne Marie Purkey, and Jeff Wonderland.

No project is realized without the support and vision of our sponsors. In this case, sincere thanks go to Amtrak and The Elizabeth Morse Charitable Trust, who have so generously helped to bring the message of the excitement and possibilities of train travel for the future to a broad public.

Martha Thorne
Associate Curator of Architecture
The Art Institute of Chicago

INDEX

PICTURE CREDITS